Property of Textbook Services

University of Wisconsin-River Falls
410 S. 3rd St., River Falls, WI 54022
Loaned subject to purchase in case of loss or damage
Due by closing time on the last day of finals
Due immediately if class is dropped or upon withdrawal
No highlighting, underlining, or writing in texts
Fines will be levied for infractions

Property of Textbook Services
University of Wisconsin-River Falls
410 S. 3rd St., River Falls, WI 54022
1. and subject to purchase in case of loss or damage
Due by closing time on the last day of finals
immediately if class is dropped or upon withdrawal
No highlighting, underlining, or writing in texts
Fines will be levied for infractions

Copyright @ 2012 by Brian Massey. All rights reserved.

Published by Content Marketing Institute, a division of Z Squared Media LLC, Cleveland, Ohio.

No part of this publication may be reproduced, stored in a retrieval system, or transmitted in any form or by any means, electronic, mechanical, photocopying, recording, scanning, or otherwise, except as permitted under section 107 or 108 of the 1976 United States Copyright Act, without the prior written permission of the publisher.

Limit of Liability/Disclaimer of Warranty: While the publisher and author have used their best efforts in preparing this book, they make no representations or warranties with respect to the accuracy or completeness of the contents of this book and specifically disclaim any implied warranties of merchantability or fitness for a particular purpose. No warranty may be created or extended by sales representatives or written sales materials. The advice and strategies contained herein may not be suitable for your situation. Neither the publisher nor the author shall be liable for any loss of profit or other commercial damages, including, but not limited to, special, incidental, consequential, or other damages.

About the Content Marketing Institute
The Content Marketing Institute (ContentInstitute.com) teaches non-media brands how to attract and retain customers through compelling, multi-channel storytelling. CMI does this through multiple offerings including the Content Marketing World event, *Chief Content Officer* magazine, and electronic and print books from leading content marketing experts.

Content Marketing Institute books are available at special quantity discounts to use as premiums and sales promotions, or for use in corporate training programs. To place a bulk order, please contact the Content Marketing Institute at info@contentinstitute.com or 888/554-2014.

ISBN 978-0-9833307-3-8
Printed in the United States of America.

YOUR CUSTOMER CREATION EQUATION

Unexpected Website Formulas of
The Conversion Scientist™

CONTENT

SOCIAL MEDIA

EMAIL

ANALYTICS

SEARCH

WEB SITE

$975

LEADS

REVENUE

BY BRIAN MASSEY

For Jeanne

No work of man ever finds
form but in pursuit of the
attention of another.

Table of Contents

When Abandonment Rates are High
Resurrecting Buyers After They Leave
View Your Checkout Process as a Service

CHAPTER 10: GETTING VISITORS PAST THE HOME PAGE 147
The Battle for the Home Page
Key Concepts in Home Page Design
Home Pages for Each of the Five Formulas
Your Designer Probably Led You Astray
Mobile Home Pages
Use Three Key Stats to Monitor Home Page Performance

CHAPTER 11: SOCIAL MEDIA: FINDING MUSIC IN THE NOISE 163
Another Attempt to Define Social Media
Two Basic Approaches to Social Media
Conversation is the Tune Your Social Network Dances To
Social Media Landing Pages
Influencers Earn Their Reputation
On-network vs. Off-network Landing Pages
The Turn: Switching from Pull to Push
Using Social Media to Charge Your Subscriber Battery
The Case for Email
Exporting Social Connections from Social Networks
Charge Your Subscription List with Facebook Applications
Control and Track Your Social Media Strategy

CHAPTER 12: ADVANCED CURRICULUM IN VISITOR STUDIES ... 179
You Don't Get a Vote
Forget What You Know About Your Customers
Identify Triggers
Compose a Customer Commentary
Target Your Best Visitors
Four Modes of Research
What Do You Want Your Visitors to Do?
Breathe Life Into Your Rock Star Personas
Where Do You Keep All of This?
No Experiment is a Failure as Long as You Learn Something From It

Introduction

There is an equation for your online business. It is different from the equation you use for your offline business. It is a unique formula, different from even your closest competitor's.

Once you discover this formula and implement it with some proficiency, your business will begin to grow in some pretty astounding ways. In fact, don't be surprised if you begin to dominate your marketplace.

In this book, you're going to learn how to find this formula. It's an equation that will turn leads into visitors, visitors into customers, and customers into advocates.

We're all familiar with the components of an offline business equation: physical stores, real employees, ads that can be touched and heard, and real customers handing us thin plastic cards that make our businesses grow. Many offline business equations often look like this:

Word-of-Mouth + Well-trained Employees + Competitive Prices = More Customers.

Our online components, however, are remarkably different. We can't see our customers. They're not coming into our stores and offices. More often, they are interacting with us through web browers that may be anywhere in the world.

Some of us have been able to develop our digital customer creation equation on our own. The rest of us must rely on experts to decipher these new digital components. Each tells us that theirs is THE solution:

Search Engine Optimization + Website = More Customers

Online Ads + Website = More Customers

Social Media = More Customers.

These equations are too simple. In an offline business, you wouldn't pay to advertise on billboards around town if your shop was hard-to-find, unattractive, or populated with rude employees.

Business equations don't have to be complex, but they have to be complete. To be complete, they must take into account strategies that get more people to the business, as well as tactics that get them to buy, return, and tell others. I wrote this book to help you understand your complete online marketing equation and how it works to create customers or clients for your business.

What You'll Learn Here

You can't drive traffic to any old website and expect good things to happen. If you're reading this, you've probably discovered this truth already.

Finding the right equation for your business will require you to take some risks, try new things, and open your mind to new ways of thinking. By the time you're finished reading this book, you will be able to:

- Change your website so that it delivers qualified customers to your business

- Identify which strategies and tactics to invest in—and which to run away from

- Manage knowledgeable experts so that they work well within your unique equation

- Create online ecosystems that naturally grow your traffic and sales simultaneously.

Whether you're new to online marketing and sales or have an existing online business, you'll walk away with actionable recommendations to find and engage more customers.

I wrote this book more for the manager than for the practitioner. It is designed to help marketing managers and business owners identify what they should be working on and impose some level of proficiency in the creation of a great online effort.

For digital marketing practitioners, I offer a vocabulary and the basic recipes that will help your clients better understand your value. You are still the chefs. This book will help your customers order intelligently from the menu.

We will start by defining the moment of truth for any online project: the point at which a visitor becomes a prospect or a prospect becomes a customer. That moment of truth is called a conversion. If your team is able to competently control conversions, your business can control the cost and effectiveness of all online expenditures, from advertising to traffic generation.

I'll show you:

- Where you are in the digital universe. Like a physical store, your website occupies a digital "footprint" amongst your customers and competitors. There are some very easy ways to understand where you are and where you can take your online business.

- How to set up a digital conversion laboratory that will tell you whether a formula is working or not. The online world is incredibly measurable. Feedback and change can come quickly if you are paying attention.

- How to use your conversion lab to answer burning questions about your business, such as, "Where are my online prospects coming from?" and "Why do people leave without connecting with us or buying something?"

- How to measure and monitor your online success, so you can stop investing in things that don't work, and double-down on those that do.

Then, I'll introduce you to:

- Five conversion formulas—aka "customer creation equations"—and show you how to choose one for your online business. This is the basic starting point from which you will develop your own unique formula to generate more leads and sales.

- Online strategies that have been proven to work for each formula and how to implement them. This will give you the power to choose online experts wisely and to properly judge their competence as they work for your business.

All of this sets the stage for an online business that has a sound foundation, free of hype and ready to deliver.

Next, you'll take a deeper look at the core components of high-converting websites: digital content, marketing batteries, landing pages, the purchase process, and home page design. These are the "knobs" that you can turn to steadily increase your conversion rates and revenues.

Finally, I'll show you how social media can increase the success of your high-converting site. Be prepared, because I'm going to dispel many of the myths that are frequently told about social networks in the digital marketing universe.

If you want to find unexpected gold in your online business and take your decision-making to a whole new level, check out the Advanced Curriculum in Visitor Studies at the back of this book. There, you'll learn about:

- The persona—a tool so powerful that once your team understands it, they will naturally make the right decisions for your online business and customers
- The four ways that visitors make buying decisions
- The three key actions that visitors can take to propel your online business forward.

What is a Conversion Scientist™?

A Conversion Scientist™ is a professional who seeks to use the scientific method to increase the life-giving conversions enjoyed by a business.

If the term "conversion" is new to you, don't be discouraged. Until a few years ago, it was new to all of us.

The irony is, that we've all been doing this for as long as we've been running websites. We just didn't call it "conversion."

The set of disciplines, strategies, tactics, and techniques that I place under the umbrella of conversion have long been hidden under the marketing concepts brought to us by Madison Avenue. These concepts include "positioning," "brand messaging," "image marketing," and "creating a feeling." They fed on a steady diet of radio, TV, and print media. There are plenty of stories of how broadcast media have made products wildly successful and lined the pockets of many an agency.

As it turns out, such values do not serve us well on the web. There is indication that most of the print, radio, and TV advertising done over the four decades of Madison Avenue's rule, in fact, did not work well for the advertiser. The reason we continue to invest in these media is that success cannot be accurately measured.

The success of broadcast media is generally measured by surveys in which an agency will interview the members of the target audience, asking them if they remember the commercial and if they're likely to buy. This implies that a large enough segment of the target audience has seen the commercial to provide a large enough sample to believe. In this scenario, businesses must use measures such as "share of mind" and "recall" to make decisions about their marketing spend.

Ultimately, it is prohibitively expensive to experiment in this media. Take Groupon, for example. They spent lavishly on their 2011 Superbowl commercials, which featured high-paid celebrities making light of serious world events. Groupon's hypothesis was that viewers would see this as quirky and humorous. They didn't. And there will be no second experiment. The budget was spent. The Superbowl passed.

To add insult to injury, Groupon really has no way of knowing if this strategy worked. Visitors may have been incensed at the callousness of the spots, but they still got Groupon burned into their minds. Maybe that led them to open and read Groupon's emails. In short, we don't know how many viewers were converted into new customers by the effort.

This is not true of online marketing. We can know with high precision how many people are seeing our ads, visiting our site, and buying from us. We can experiment to see what makes more visitors buy—and what chases more of them away. This process is more akin to science than art, and it is a core advantage for those businesses investing in online media.

Hence, the term Conversion Scientist.

I don't have to convince you that you want to get more leads and customers from the stream of visitors coming to your website. You already knew that or you wouldn't be investing in online marketing. I doubt you'd be reading this book.

What I must get through to you—and what I had to learn myself—is that the web offers us a medium fundamentally different from TV, radio, and print. We no longer have to plant subversive messages in people's minds as they read magazines, watch TV, and listen to the radio. Instead, we can engage them closer to the time when they're going to spend money to solve a problem, and very accurately measure their responses to the messages we put in front of them.

In short, we no longer have to send our messages out and pray that they're persuasive. We can measure their effectiveness, learn from the results, and get better at giving our online prospects what they need.

It has only been in the last six or seven years that I've given the term conversion to that which I do. Like you, I had been the business owner, entrepreneur, corporate marketer, search engine consultant, or agency exec treating the Internet like any other broadcast medium.

Since the turn of this century, we have invested most heavily in driving traffic to our sites. More visitors means more sales, right? As competition heats up, competitors are driving up the price of paid search ads. They are crowding us off of "page one," requiring us to redouble our efforts to keep our rankings high.

Google, Bing, and Yahoo control this ecosystem, and benefit from higher prices and taller barriers to entry. They encourage this scarcity of traffic because they can charge more for scarce resources.

The only way to get off this treadmill of scarcity is to focus on things that you control. You control your web pages, your email, your content. *You* **control the components of your business that make visitors convert into prospects and buyers.**

It's Time to Improve Conversion Efficiency

As you'll see in this book, efficiencies on the conversion side of the equation do more than save money—they are a lever that raises the effectiveness of all marketing. They reduce the cost of acquiring new leads and sales.

So even if you face a well-funded large competitor in your online marketing efforts, you'll be able to effectively outspend them with a much smaller budget when you focus on conversion efficiencies.

Let me put that another way: Small increases in your conversion rate result in big savings on marketing because the cost of acquiring each customer goes down.

In almost 20 years of online marketing, and most recently as the Conversion Scientist, I have been privileged to have built, co-created, or consulted with hundreds of businesses on their websites.

For more than a year, I have spent every Friday on the phone with business after business doing free consultations. Almost 100 businesses have taken advantage of this offering.

I have presented to thousands of students all across North America, offering attendees a live site review, in which I publicly point out blocks to conversion and missed opportunities. I've heard the stories, and regardless of the industry, they are consistently similar.

We are all making the same mistakes over and over—mistakes that keep our marketing costs high and our conversion rates low.

See if any of these stories sounds familiar to you:

The Web Deserter

You have learned that web developers are not finishers. They have managed your expectations poorly and do not have the resources to finish their work. At the time you're sprinting for the finish line, they start pulling back.

The Search Engine Obfuscator

Your search engine optimization (SEO) firm delivers monthly reports containing graph after graph all pointed up and to the right just like they promised. However, you're not seeing the new business, sales, and prospects that you would expect from a higher ranking and more traffic.

The "Pretty Sells" Designer

The bulk of your web budget went to the design firm you hired. They delivered a nice-looking site, but relied on you to make most of the design decisions and deliver the content. Everyone loves the site, but it isn't doing anything for the business.

Most likely you picked up this book because you are a character in one or more of these stories. You are here because you've paid someone to drive traffic to your site, but you have little to show for it.

How can a business like yours with such great offerings at excellent prices seem so invisible to the people coming to your site? How can you be doing so well in offline sales and so poorly online?

These are very good questions.

There are two overarching factors at work here, and this book will equip you to deal with both:

- What you know about how people make buying decisions in the offline world is betraying you in your online efforts
- The experts who understand the online world don't know enough about your business to effectively market to your prospects.

In other words, you're asking the people building your online business to do things that don't work on the web, and they don't know your business well enough to stop you.

To remedy this situation, you need to understand enough about the online world to effectively manage the team, and you need them to intimately understand who you are marketing to.

Here are a few questions that will let you do a quick self-analysis of your web development attitudes. Check the statements that are true for a site you've worked on:

- ❑ Most of the money spent on the website went to the designer or design firm.
- ❑ Most of the internal discussion was about the look and feel of the site.

❑ It was important that the site look unique to differentiate the business from the competition.

❑ The copy for the site was reviewed and edited by management (if not written by them).

❑ Most of the pages on the site talk about the company or its products.

❑ The primary navigation requires visitors to follow a logical path down to the product or service they're interested in.

❑ I believe that my company logo and tagline are crucial elements of my website.

Okay—how many check marks are there?

If there are none (or one), you're not being honest with yourself.

If most of the boxes are checked, you can count your site among the 90 percent on the web that are beautiful homages to their businesses but are delivering horrible results.

If your reaction is, "Of course, most of them are checked. Why wouldn't they be?" don't worry. You have built a brochure site that will give visitors a good impression. The bad news is that it won't make the cash register ring because these are not the most important issues if you want your site to generate leads and sales. The good news is that you probably have an attractive site on which to start building the site you really want: a high-converting, profitable, lead-generating, self-perpetuating online property.

I assure you that, despite any previous missteps, you have what it takes to do this.

The first thing we must do is unlearn some of the truisms handed to us by Madison Avenue, by our designers and developers, and by our experiences in other sales channels. Everyone involved meant well, but we are all suffering from the same disease.

We will no longer be led by the blind.

We must accept the fact that conversion is first and foremost about measuring results. Analytics gives us information about our prospects and customers that we can find in no other way.

We must acknowledge that conversion is a collection of strategies, not just a bunch of landing pages, forms, buttons, and shopping carts. We can choose more wisely where to spend our marketing dollars and when to let go of tactics that just don't work.

This book is for inquiring, curious business owners and corporate marketers who will make insightful decisions for their online properties if given the right information.

Let's go get it.

Chapter 1
What is Conversion Science?

Conversion consultant Michael Drew asks a very telling question of online businesses and marketers: *What if 98 percent of the people who visited a grocery left without buying anything?*

Yet, the vast majority of websites are able to turn only two or three percent of visitors into prospects or buyers. That means that 98 percent of people are leaving these sites without taking any action.

To put it another way, on average, sites have a two or three percent *conversion rate*. Most sites convert at even lower rates.

If the term *conversion* is new to you, I am very excited that you're reading this book. The reason I'm so excited is because I love to open people's eyes. Once you understand conversion, you'll never look at your website the same way again.

Even better, I predict that your business will never be the same. If you're willing to commit to the Internet as a powerful marketing and business growth tool, you will gain a strong advantage over your slower-moving competitors.

It's like the word *constellation*.

When we were young we looked up at the night sky and we saw stars scattered all about. At some point someone introduced us to the term *constellation* and suddenly, the night sky became something altogether different. It became a place filled with stories, characters, and myths. Many believe that the constellation you are born under will influence your entire life.

You may not have known it, but conversion has been a part of your business since the first day you had a website. Just as the stars took on new meaning with the introduction of the word *constellation*, so too will your website take on new meaning as you explore the concepts and practices of conversion science.

Conversion Defined

The most common definition of conversion is a *transformation*. In the case of the Internet, we seek to *transform* a visitor into a *customer*. When somebody buys from us, we call that a *conversion*; we have converted a visitor into a customer. However, conversion has a broader set of meanings for many businesses.

Turning visitors into buyers is an important conversion for an *online store*. For a company selling to other businesses, such as accounting services or software companies, *lead generation* is the most important conversion the website can deliver. These sites seek to convert visitors into *prospects*.

In fact, there are several conversions that can and will occur for your business on the Internet. From the first time somebody hears about your company to the time they begin telling others about you, there are several transformations they will go through:

- *Strangers* convert to *suspects* when they see your advertising
- *Suspects* convert to *prospects* when they identify themselves to you
- *Prospects* convert to *customers* when they buy
- *Customers* convert to *users* when they use your product or service
- *Users* convert to *repeat buyers* when they buy from you again
- *Users* convert to *advocates* when they share their experience of your product or service with others.

For some businesses, all of this can be done on the web. Businesses that advertise online and deliver an online service can complete each transformation through their website. Brick and mortar retailers may only be able to identify prospects or generate leads with their website.

Don't be overwhelmed by all of these conversions. Your business is already doing this, but it may not be doing it well. This book will help you identify when these conversions occur, and give you the tools you need to get more of your visitors to convert to subscribers, leads, and sales.

Conversions are not only great for your business, but also for your visitors. Each conversion means that a visitor has found what he was looking for and that he has chosen you as his source to solve a problem or to entertain him. This is the very definition of a win-win scenario. **When Internet surfers find what they're looking for on your site, your business will grow.**

The Scientific Method Isn't Scary

You use the scientific method every day. You just don't use it consciously.

You use it every time you cook something new for dinner. You start by *evaluating* your family and developing a *hypothesis:* "My family will enjoy this new entrée for dinner because they like other recipes with these ingredients." You then conceive of an *experiment:* "I will prepare the entrée for dinner and measure my family's response."

Next you prepare the dinner and serve it. As your family eats, you monitor important *measurements.* You watch their eyebrows for signs of appreciation. You watch their mouths for signs of smiles. You listen closely for the telltale utterances of "mmmmm" and "delicious!"

Perhaps you also throw in a post-experiment survey by asking, "What did you think?"

The results will tell you what action to take. If the response is positive, you'll add the new entrée to your regular menu rotation. If the response is negative, you can try to figure out what your family disliked, and select a different recipe in your search for a menu with variety and nutrition.

This is the *scientific* method.

- *Evaluate* existing information
- Develop a *hypothesis*
- Test your hypothesis using an *experiment*
- *Measure* your results
- *Take action* on the new information.

Each step in this process is critical, and chances are you're not considering them when making changes to your website. With a little discipline, you could be learning critical lessons about what your visitors want when they come to your site, and how to convert more of them into prospects and customers for your business.

Ignore the Scientific Method at Your Peril

Tom Jackson had a nice online business booking helicopter skiing vacations for well-off adventurers. He wrote to me complaining that his old "dated, awkward, wordy, but it's working" website at HeliskiingReview.com was outperforming his newer, better looking, better organized website at Heliski.com (see Figure 1.1). In fact, the old site generated 12 times more paid trips than the new site did through his peak season.

Had Tom done what most businesses do, and simply replaced the old website with the new one, he would have been put out of business.

By keeping both sites live, Tom had inadvertently employed the scientific method.

Based on his *evaluation* of other sites and the input of an experienced web designer, Tom developed the *hypothesis* that a professionally designed website would generate more leads and bookings for his business.

His *experiment* was to create this "new and improved" website and see if it would generate more leads and entice more visitors to book a trip with him.

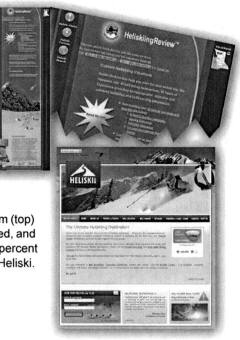

Figure 1.1: HeliskiingReview.com (top) was thought to be too wordy, dated, and awkward. But it generated 1,200 percent more sales than the redesigned Heliski. com (bottom).

In the final analysis, both sites received about the same amount of traffic. About the same number of visitors completed his request form on both sites. But **those who visited the old site were far more likely to actually book a trip than those who visited the new site.**

So much had changed between the two sites that it was difficult to tell which aspects of the old site had the greatest impact on leads and trip bookings. In my analysis, I thought that the "wordy" copy on the old site appealed more to visitors who were actively considering a heliskiing vacation. I felt the *calls to action* were clearer and that the *navigation* was simpler, which helped visitors decide where to go. I also believed that the domain name HeliskiingReview.com drew more *qualified traffic* from the search engines, because serious shoppers want reviews.

Based on his sales data, Tom took *action*. He chose to leave the old site up and experiment with the new site in the hopes of increasing its effectiveness. By making changes more deliberately, Tom has already begun to get better results from the new site.

Measuring Conversion

One of the reasons why businesses neglect conversion when building their websites is that they don't understand how to measure their sites effectively. They look only at the number of sales or leads they're getting, and this is not enough.

An online store may receive 10 sales per day, and that may mean the site is profitable. However, if they knew that they were getting 1,000 visitors a day, they would realize that their site is losing 990 potential buyers every day.

For this reason, we measure the conversion *rate* of a site.

The conversion rate is the number of conversions divided by the number of visitors who come for a given period of time.

By expressing the conversion rate as a percentage, we can measure the site's effectiveness regardless of how many people visit or buy.

In the above example, the conversion rate would be 10 buyers divided by 1,000 visitors, or one percent (10/1,000 = one percent).

If the number of people visiting drops to 500 one day, but 10 still buy, the conversion rate increases to two percent (10/500 = two percent).

If you only looked at sales, you would miss the fact that your traffic is dropping—and that your site is converting more efficiently.

Changing Your Conversion Rate

An increase in conversion rate from one percent to just two percent allows the business to generate the same sales from half the visits. This illustrates the peculiar math of conversion.

Because the conversion rate is a fraction, there are two ways you can increase it:

1. Get more visitors to take action, or
2. Reduce the number of visitors to the site.

Figure 1.2: Two ways to increase your conversion rate.

Your eyebrows should have gone up a bit with that last one, "Reduce the number of visitors." The catch here is that, if you reduce the traffic to your site, you cannot let the number of people taking action fall.

Let's think this through.

To increase your conversion rate by reducing your traffic, you must bring *better qualified* visitors—those who are ready to take action. If you advertise in the wrong places, you will generate lots of visitors to your site who aren't really interested in what you offer. However, well-targeted advertising may bring fewer visitors, but entice those who are much more interested in taking action.

To restate this, there are two ways to increase your conversion rate:

- Get more visitors to take action, or
- Bring in fewer unqualified visitors.

Which strategy is more important? To get the high conversion rates you want, you must master both. It doesn't matter how well-qualified your traffic is if you're chasing them away with poor conversion strategies and bad execution. People are coming to your site already. Let's figure out how to delight these visitors, and then we'll open the spigot of well-qualified traffic.

Making the Science Work for Your Business

While you may not have used the term "conversion," you've certainly wanted web visitors to become buyers. Therefore, your site most likely:

- Is pleasing to the eye
- Covers the most important points about your products or services
- Features an attractive logo and an enticing tagline for your business
- Tells people how to reach you.

Madison Avenue has taught us that this should be enough. They've lead us to believe that, if we are clever with a turn of phrase, look unique or innovative, and create an emotional experience, that we will be successful in turning strangers into customers. While there is some evidence that this approach works with TV commercials, billboards, and magazine ads, it has proven to be insufficient on the web.

Most of the businesses I've worked with have come to me with conversion rates below two percent (and an alarming number have been below one percent). These businesses are investing hard-earned money to get visitors to come to their websites, primarily through advertising and search engine marketing. All of this money and effort is being spent so that less than two out of every 100 visitors take action. Yikes.

Small Increases in Conversion Deliver Big Increases for Your Business

What if you put one of the recommendations in this book to work on your site and made a change that would get just one more person out of every 100 to buy from you? So instead of getting two out of every 100, you got three to convert? It doesn't sound like a big deal, does it?

But by increasing your conversion rate from two to three out of 100, **your sales would grow by about *50 percent*.** Moving your conversion rate from two percent to three percent delivers 150 percent of revenue.

This is the magical mathematics of conversion. Small increases in conversion rates result in big increases for your business.

Now consider the businesses that are committed to optimizing their websites for conversion. These businesses convert 10 percent, 20 percent, or more of their visitors into customers. What impact would it have on your bottom line if your website had a conversion rate of 10 percent or more?

I can tell you this: it would place you at the forefront of your industry. It would create a marketing asset so powerful that competitors would have difficulty keeping up. It would increase your profit, decrease your marketing costs, and give you the freedom to delight your customers in ways that most businesses only dream of.

If your site is not converting well, it is because you have ignored the science of online marketing. There are formulas that govern online marketing—formulas that produce measurable results and have been proven on website after website. You do not need to reinvent these formulas.

The Incredible Measurable Web

The reason that the scientific method is so powerful in online marketing is that your website is controlled by a computer, and computers are very good at keeping track of things. The computer knows how many people are coming to your website. It knows which pages visitors are looking at. It knows when people leave and when they take action. Through your computer, you can get vital information on your visitors every day.

With this information, you can determine if a change increased or decreased your conversion rate. From there the approach is simple: Keep the things that work and throw away those that don't. After a period of trying new things and keeping the changes that work, your business should enjoy higher conversion rates and lower marketing costs, both of which will translate into more success and more growth.

Market Research is a Collection of Hypotheses, Not Answers

Whatever you believe about the people coming to your site is probably wrong. Even if you have done extensive surveying, focus groups, and interviews, you most likely don't have an accurate picture of your web visitors. Here's why:

- When people come to your website, they are coming for completely different reasons than if they were walking into a store. Unless you understand their intentions, you are working with the wrong answers.
- People can't tell you the truth about their actions. In his book *Consumer.ology,* Philip Graves calls market research a "myth." It turns out that people don't really know why they do the things they do. In fact, they will often do the opposite of what they claim.

So, if you can't use your research, what should you do?

Treat the research as hypotheses, not answers.

A *hypothesis* is an educated guess and part of the scientific method. It is not simply called a "guess," because the word "hypothesis" implies a "tentative insight," and "a concept that is not yet verified."

In other words, a guess is a shot in the dark. A hypothesis, on the other hand, can be tested to see if it is true.

I'll show you how to set up a digital conversion lab that will put an end to your guessing, letting you test hypotheses right on your own website.

This is how you dominate your industry. You come up with a set of assumptions about what will make visitors buy more on your site and then test your assumptions. Your hypotheses may be very similar to your competitors' guesses. However, you are going to find out which are really true and which are not.

Your competitors may be reading this book, too. Whoever learns the fastest wins.

Look at Every Change as an Experiment

If your intention is to steadily increase the effectiveness of your website, you're going to have to look at things a bit differently. You'll have to view every change to your site—no matter how small—as an experiment. Each change must have a hypothesis and a way to measure results.

Consider the next change you are going to make. It could be posting a new article, adding some new products, or adding keywords to your copy for search engine optimization (SEO). It doesn't matter what the change is. There are two key questions to ask to implement the scientific method:

1. *"What do I think will change when I implement this?"* This is your hypothesis.
2. *"How will I measure that change?"*

Your answers should be as specific as possible. Do you expect to get more traffic? Do you expect more people to convert on your site? How will you measure traffic and conversions?

By the time you're finished reading this book, you'll know exactly what questions to ask your web development team to ensure that they're keeping conversion science in mind as they plan changes.

In the next chapter, you'll learn how you and your team can measure and prove—or disprove—your hypotheses.

Chapter 2
Your Digital Conversion Laboratory

While you were reading the last chapter, a few questions probably came to mind:

"If my conversion rate is the number of actions divided by visits, how do I know how many visits my site gets?"

"The scientific method says I should test a hypothesis and then evaluate the results. Where do these results come from?"

"I manage my business by walking around. How do I walk around my webite?"

You're going to answer these questions in your own conversion laboratory. I think you're going to love it. Think of it as your Bat Cave, your Fortress of Solitude, or your presidential situation room.

In other words, it's high-tech and cool. But that doesn't mean it has to be difficult to build.

Do not underestimate the power you have to monitor and control a digital world that is, in many ways, as real as the one you are walking around in.

Like the laboratories you might find a chemist in, your conversion lab will have the tools you need to conduct and monitor a wide variety of experiments:

- *Raw materials*—the **content** that forms the compounds you'll work with
- *Sensitive measurement tools to accurately gauge your results*—the **analytics** you'll collect
- *Beakers, flasks, and test tubes*—the web pages, inboxes, social pages, and other **channels** in which you'll conduct your experiments.

You don't have to invest in a facility for your lab. It lives on your desktop and on the servers of service providers. Most of your lab work will be done in a browser with some support from spreadsheet software.

In your lab, you will detect shifts in the marketplace. You will watch people surf the web like ants between glass. You will control assets on servers across the globe. You will stare into the tumbling symbols of the Matrix and begin to understand them.

And your business decisions will improve tremendously.

Let's look at an example of how one company used its digital lab to outperform its bigger competitors.

Figure 2.1: Your digital conversion lab will have all the tools you need to conduct and monitor a wide variety of experiments.

Extra Space Runs Rings Around the Competition

When you have more stuff than you have space, you rent a self-storage unit from one of many facilities found in every city. No matter how small the town in which you live, there will be one or more of these mini warehouses, ready to lend you some room.

The new house isn't ready? The wife kicked you out? School is out for the summer? They've got space for you. For the most part, this industry is dominated by small, local operations owning only two or three facilities. However, elephants dance in this industry, as they probably do in yours.

The largest, Public Storage, manages more than 2,000 locations across America. However, a relatively small competitor, Extra Space Storage Inc., has been able to outperform this giant, growing to 882 locations. Extra Space may be less than half the size of Public Storage, but their stores are more efficient. They attract new renters more cost-effectively, who stay with them longer, paying more for the privilege.

Extra Space has led in "average same-store performance" for **25 consecutive quarters**. That's over six years. "Average same-store performance" simply means that the facilities they own and manage stay rented at profitable prices.

The web is one of the reasons they are winning, quarter after quarter.

A few years ago, Extra Space's competitors were assuming that little had changed in the way people find self-storage facilities, relying primarily on signage, repeat business, referrals, and the Yellow Pages. Extra Space was busy doing research. That research showed that customers were increasingly relying on the Internet. As a result, Extra Space began to invest more heavily in their website and pay closer attention to their analytics.

Today, Extra Space makes decisions based on real data. They have invested in the tools and the staff to maximize the role their website plays in getting and retaining renters. They know a great deal about their customers through their website—and you can, too.

Adding Analytics to Your Lab

An ant farm is an environment in which we can observe the lifecycle of a small colony of ants. Likewise, your digital marketing lab is going to turn your website into an environment in which you can observe your web visitors.

An ant farm is typically composed of two panes of glass spaced slightly wider than an ant tunnel. Your website will also be given something equivalent to glass walls, in the form of *analytics*.

The space between the glasses is filled with dirt. This is where the ants will build their tunnels and live. Similarly, your website is filled with content through which your visitors will find their own path, guided by your site navigation and site search.

Analytics software gives us the ability to watch as our ants dig and tunnel. We can watch as they forage above their slice of ground. We can see when and where they are active and inactive. We can identify which tunnels they visit more often and how they use the different chambers they create.

We are actually going to turn your entire website into an ant farm.

The word "analytics" is one of those terms you can use when you want to sound smarter than everyone else. It has an intimidation factor. However, if you realize that analytics are simply answers to your questions, you may find them less scary.

The key to understanding analytics, then, is knowing what questions to ask. When analytics provide answers about your business, they go from being geeky to being very cool. They are the eyes and ears of your website.

Analytics work like this: Every time someone comes to your website, you count them as one visitor. Then at the end of each day, you can see how many visitors you had. Most analytics software will display a graph of visitors over time.

There are a number of companies that sell analytics software, with more products being released every year. However, Google offers a free solution, appropriately called *Google Analytics,* which is capable of answering almost any question you can ask about a website.

Google Analytics is an online service that will track your site's visitors, telling you the number of times they visit and every page they look at. Plus, it will tell you where visitors are coming from (e.g., search engines, other sites, ads).

Choosing an Analytics Service

There are a number of services that will track your site analytics for you. Clicky (GetClicky.com) is a popular one known for the simplicity of its user interface.

Enterprises use high-end solutions like Adobe Site Catalyst, Coremetrics, and Webtrends. These are not free, and they are more complex to set up and implement. However, they offer advanced reporting that major enterprises desire.

My preference is Google Analytics. It offers a very full feature set, it is easy to install on your pages, and it's free. A low-cost alternative with a funny name is Woopra (Woopra.com).

You may find yourself advertising with Google Adwords at some point, if you are not already. At present, Google is the king of search advertising, and Google Analytics is integrated into the Adwords platform.

Once your team has installed Google Analytics or something similar, the software will begin collecting information about your site. If you combine this information with insights about your competition, you will begin to understand the forces at work on your business.

What Do Analytics Measure?

The stream of visitors to your site is called "traffic," a term borrowed from retail stores that desire "foot traffic." It is the job of your analytics service to measure this traffic.

Visitors are counted only once, no matter how many times they visit. We also call these "unique visitors" or "uniques" for short.

Each visitor can make multiple visits to your site. They may visit on Monday and then again on Tuesday. Weeks may pass between visits. Nonetheless, it will be helpful to know how many times people are visiting your business online over time.

Each time a person visits, she may view more than one page of your website. These are called *pageviews.* When the average number of pageviews increases, you can imply that visitors are more interested—or more *engaged*—in your site. This can be a positive sign.

Visits, Visitors, or Pageviews?

So which is most important to count: visitors, visits, or pageviews? It depends on your business.

If you sell advertising on your site, you'll want to track pageviews, because each page that is viewed carries ads. A pageview is a good measurement of *impressions,* which is what advertisers are looking for.

If you run an online store, and people buy from you

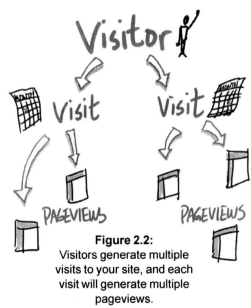

Figure 2.2:
Visitors generate multiple visits to your site, and each visit will generate multiple pageviews.

over and over, then visits are the most important thing to watch for, since each visit can mean a new sale regardless of whether it is a new visitor or a repeat customer.

If you're using your website to generate leads for your sales team, then visitors will be most important, since you can only get one lead from each visitor.

In practice, most of our measurements will be based on visits, as this is the most common unit used by Google Analytics.

Analytics is primarily a database of the pages that have been opened by any and all of the visitors to your site. The software stores the date and time that each page was opened, along with other interesting information about the visitor, such as:

- The type of computer or mobile device they are using
- The type of web browser they are using
- The search keyword that brought them to the page (if they came through a search engine)
- The web address of the page they came from
- The resolution of their computer screen
- The IP address of their computer.

You will be able to answer some pretty interesting questions with all of this data.

Lies, Damn Lies, and Analytics

Before you embark on your quest to understand your online universe, I want to make one thing very clear: all of the data we collect are *estimates*. You will never know the truth about the visitors to your website.

What you'll want to strive for in your digital conversion lab is "consistent inaccuracy." Everything is relative. In other words, it's more important that you measure things the same way day after day than work to get the most accurate measurement. For a number of reasons, pin-point accuracy is too hard.

Of course, your analytics must *correlate* to reality. If your sales go up, your analytics should reflect a similar increase in purchases. If you measure things *consistently* over time, you'll be able to learn something from the changes you make to your site.

You'll learn how to apply analytics information in Chapter 5, *Catching Conversions.*

Spy on Your Competitors

It's important to know who's winning the web game in your industry. You'll want to know which of your competitors is getting their feet wet and who's still sitting back. Get started by checking out Compete at Compete.com.

With the free version, you can insert three of your competitors' web addresses. Compete will then provide its estimate of the number of *unique visitors* that it estimates may have come to each site over the last year. The accuracy of this data is questionable, so you can use Quantcast (Quantcast.com) for a second opinion.

Quantcast lets you enter your company's domain to generate a graph of the "people" who have visited. You can then add your competitors' sites one at a time. "People" should roughly correlate to Compete's "unique visitors" metric. If you want to explore your digital marketplace from more angles, check out a third service, Alexa (www. alexa.com).

Do Your Competitors Have Conversion Labs?

It might be interesting to know if your competitors are using analytics or any of the other conversion lab equipment I'm going to introduce you to in this book. A browser plugin called Ghostery (Ghostery.com) can tell you.

After you install Ghostery, go to a competing website and click on the little ghost icon. You will be presented with a list of services installed on that site. Most of the analytics packages will be listed, if present. Many of the things on the list—ad networks, website testing tools, and social media widgets—will not be familiar to you. Don't worry. Each item has a link to more information. If you find out that your competition has analytics and testing software installed, you know you need to turn up your own game.

There are spy tools that let you snoop on the search keywords your competitors are buying, sites that offer statistics on your industry, and many more. These can be found through the book website, or simply scan this QR code with your smartphone.

Scan here to learn more about spy tools and other sites that will help you gather statistical information.

MyConversionLab.com

A Note about Browsers

Your web browser will host much of the equipment in your digital conversion lab. As of this writing, the people who build many of the online tools you'll be using don't use Internet Explorer. There are many possible reasons for this, but I won't speculate here. For this reason, Firefox (Firefox.com) seems to be the browser with the greatest level of compatibility and the most advanced extensions and plugins. If you are on Internet Explorer or Safari for the Mac, I recommend installing Firefox for your digital conversion lab browser.

Now that you've begun to set up your digital conversion lab, let's take a look at the kind of website you have and whether the formula you are currently using is serving your business as well as it could be.

Chapter 3
What Kind of Website Should You Be Running?

When a website isn't delivering for the business, the fault can often be traced to the context in which the site was developed.

"We need a better website," is the statement that often gets things started. This is the wrong way to start, as it typically leads to a complete redesign with little regard for what is working and what is not.

This is the equivalent of a retailer saying, "We need a store!" before going into business. The type of store will be different for a men's clothier than it will for an auto parts store.

The men's store will have its inventory out for visitors to see and touch. The auto parts store will warehouse parts in back. Both will require knowledgeable sales clerks to ascertain visitors' needs and direct them to the right suits and parts.

Their overall strategies will be different as well. The men's store will likely be located in a mall. This wouldn't work so well for an auto parts store, where the parking lot is used as a repair shop. Batteries and windshield wipers are typically replaced right out front.

The lesson here is that all businesses are different and your website should be unique. But at the same time, your site must follow expected conventions—conventions that your visitors rely on to find their way to solutions to their problems.

While our men's clothier may not be successful copying an auto parts store, they will follow many of the same techniques a women's clothing store uses. Merchandise will be out for patrons to browse. Dressing rooms will be available.

This is what shoppers expect. Any deviation may drive customers away.

What kind of site are your prospects expecting to find? What strategies will lead to positive experiences as measured by conversions?

The Five Primary Conversion Formulas

To date, I've never found a website that has not fit into one of the following five **primary conversion formulas:**

1. The brochure
2. The publication
3. The online store
4. The consultative site
5. The online service.

Your site will most naturally fit into one of these patterns, but choosing the one that is right for your business may not be as obvious as it seems.

See if you can pick your pattern.

The Brochure Site

The brochure has been with us for centuries. Its use in print enabled companies to present themselves to prospective customers in a wide variety of settings. It could be left behind by salespeople, sent through the mail, placed on brochure stands, set on store counters, distributed at trade shows, and stuck under windshield wipers.

As such, the brochure has had to work very hard to explain the features of a product or service and address any primary objections. Because it was used in so many ways, a brochure had to support a variety of communication styles. It had to communicate visually, in writing, and through its very design.

The first conversion that a brochure could accomplish was to have a prospect stick it in his or her pocket. The last conversion it could accomplish was to have him or her contact the company for more information.

A website doesn't have the limitations of a brochure. With a website, you aren't limited to six panels. You can provide pages and pages of information for visitors to explore. However, if you look across the web today, you get the feeling that the Internet is one great big digital brochure stand.

The majority of websites today follow the conventions of the brochure blindly:

- Copy that focuses solely on the features and benefits of the offering and the positive attributes of the company
- Gratuitous images—often stock photographs—selected to make the company seem more likeable
- A logical top-down structure with navigation that inevitably includes "Our Products," "About Us," and "Contact Us."

This is unfortunate because web visitors want so much more—and it's so easy to give them what they want in the digital world.

When is an Online Brochure Appropriate?

The advantage of the brochure site is that it's safe. Like a runway model, its only job is to display the product in its best light. With an impeccable design, copy that ruffles no feathers, and safe images, there is no fear in bringing prospects to the site.

It will be resoundingly approved by your management.

Choose the brochure formula if you do not perceive the web as an important channel for online leads or sales. It does a fantastic job of:

- Supporting salespeople, who can refer prospects to it with little fear
- Providing contact information for the company
- Helping visitors find the location of your stores
- Supporting your company's brand image.

If you have an established brand in your industry and people are looking for you, your brochure site will generate calls, store traffic, and even the occasional "Contact Us" form submission.

If you want to do more for your business, consider one of the other four formulas.

The Publication Site

Like the brochure, sites that publish original or curated information enjoy a rich ancestry in the print medium. Book publishers, newspapers, magazines, circulars, and newsletters have been a staple of our lives, offering information for every interest imaginable.

The Internet has put the ability to publish into the hands of every man, woman, and child. In fact, it's been the weblog that has helped transform the web from a digital brochure stand into something more interesting to prospects and customers.

Think for a moment about the following sites: CNN.com, FoxNews. com, YouTube, Oprah.com, TheOnion.com, NASA.gov—and your blog. Yes, the publication formula is found far and wide across the web.

Despite the variety of formats and media, these sites have some very important things in common. A publication site:

- Delivers the goods in the form of online content, either original or collected
- Makes money through subscriptions, through donations, by selling advertising, or all of the above.

Take a hard look at this site formula even if you don't consider your business to be a publisher.

The Online Store

There is nothing we want or need that we cannot acquire online. Likewise, there is nothing that we can't sell online as long as we can draw and convert visitors (and provided we're not breaking any laws!).

Whenever someone has said, "No one will ever buy that online," someone else has said, "Oh, really?" and proceeded to prove them wrong.

The term "online store" is a bit of a misnomer, as it implies sites that sell a catalog of products. In truth, a one-page website with one product has much in common with a catalog ecommerce site.

For the sake of our conversion formulas, an online store is defined as one where:

- Visitors can purchase a product online using any agreed-upon currency
- The site does not provide the product or service directly, as would the online service or publication formulas.

Examples include eBay, Amazon, Etsy, information marketers, and book authors. Given the breadth of this category, it seems incredible that these sites follow a single pattern. Keep reading and it will all make sense.

The Consultative Site

This formula is specifically designed to support your sales team through the long sales cycles often found in business-to-business (B2B) transactions.

Actually, this formula is primarily designed to support the champions at prospective client companies until a decision to buy has been reached. Therefore, it isn't your sales team that should dictate what goes on the site, but your prospects. Of course, your salespeople can give you the best insight as to what information these champions need in order to sell your products/services within their companies (at least the successful salespeople can).

The consultative site has the following characteristics:

- The company delivers a complex or expensive product or service that requires a consultative sell
- Multiple people will be involved in the decision to buy.

These criteria almost guarantee that each sale will require days, weeks, or months to complete from the first visit. However, this isn't always the case.

At first glance, it appears that Excitations.com sells gift experiences for personal and corporate giving (see Figure 3.1). This sounds like an online store, right? Well, a closer look reveals that they sell *guidance* for unique experiences, including fighter jet rides, horseback excursions, and gourmet indulgences.

Excitations.com offers the types of features you might find on a consultative site, such as the "Gift Finder." Indeed, "Find a Gift" is the most prominent navigation item on the site.

Excitations might have chosen a primary navigation design more like a store, in which gifts are segmented into categories, but they didn't. They chose navigation that focuses on helping buyers decide on a gift.

As you'll see, there are different conversion strategies to be followed depending on the chosen formula. Ultimately, Excitations may choose to mix and match strategies from both the online store and consultative formulas.

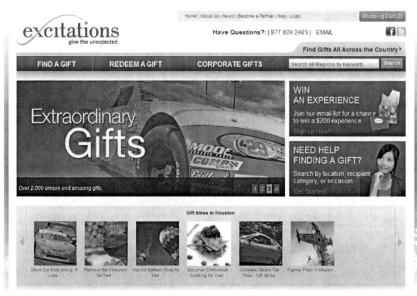

Figure 3.1: Is Excitations.com an online store for gifts or a consultative site for gift seekers?

The Online Service

What was once called "Web 2.0" has given way to "the cloud." Applications that once required the purchase of desktop software have been replaced by sites that provide such services through your favorite browser.

I can't imagine running a small business without services like Freshbooks, MyFax, Timebridge, and Google Docs. Enterprises are also getting into the act, with online marketing automation systems like Silverpop, Manticore, and Eloqua, which are integrated with online customer relationship management (CRM) services such as Salesforce and Highrise.

We no longer "start" with the Windows start button or "find" applications with Apple's Finder. Instead, we simply open a browser and a host of solutions are there among our bookmarks.

We do our finances, socialize, organize ideas, manage our job search, share travel plans, and recruit college students all from the comfort of our browsers.

In every category, there are multiple online services competing for our attention: social networking, dating, to-do lists, collaboration tools, bookmarking services, calendars, and more.

As you will see, your digital conversion lab will be composed of many online service solutions.

The online service formula is defined as:

- Visitors purchase access to the site online
- The product is delivered online by the service, in a browser, a mobile app, or desktop application.

The challenge these sites face is the ubiquitous "freemium" model, in which a set of features is given away for free, and more advanced features require a payment to use. Thus, there are two conversions that must take place: converting visitors to free users, and then converting free users to premium users. We discuss strategies for these conversions, and for all of the conversion formulas, in the next chapter.

Which Conversion Formula Do You Use?

You may think that your website fits squarely into one of the five formulas—brochure, publisher, online store, consultative site, or online service. However, it's not always so cut and dry.

For example, YouTube is a publisher of video content, but it also provides a service to video authors, enabling them to edit their videos and create channels. Is this not an online service model as well?

Hoover's Online offers information that helps salespeople qualify and penetrate new accounts. The service can be expensive, so it requires multiple decision-makers to be involved. Should Hoover's follow a consultative site model? Is their company research capability an online service, or are they a publication formula that publishes company intelligence?

Hoover's uses strategies from more than one formula. They offer a free trial to engage visitors. They present their reports like the products found in an online store. They also sell advertising, as a publication would.

Be warned: A mash-up of strategies like this is difficult to implement. A site like Hoovers Online can feel schizophrenic with no clear identity. Ads and pop-ups will interrupt visitors, stealing attention away from the mainline business product.

Are you using several different strategies? Or are you truly following the pattern for one formula? Is it time to consider something different?

There are three primary reasons why you might be better off using another formula:

1. Your current site is using the wrong formula.

If your team followed the advice of a design firm, odds are they chose a formula they were familiar with, that was easy to sell to management, but that doesn't serve the business.

The most common site built for a B2B company is the brochure. However, as I've pointed out, this formula is not going to generate leads, qualify them, and support them through a long sales process.

2. Your customers want you to be something different.

When you understand what brings visitors to your site, you may find that their needs dictate a different approach. For example, many

Figure 3.2: Musical artists Vienna Teng and Alex Wong give their fans what they want: stories and connection. This is the job of a publication.

Figure 3.3: Hipmunk takes an online service approach compared to Orbitz's (top) online sales approach.

rock stars, singers, and indie bands sell their music on the web. This would lead us to believe that they should follow the online store formula.

However, if you examine why fans visit a site, it is often to find out where the band is playing, to read the lyrics to a song they just heard, to connect with their favorite band members, or to see what others are saying about this music that they love so much.

This is a publisher formula (see Figure 3.2). The primary goal is to get visitors to subscribe to the site's content so they will come back again and again. And, yes, it's perfectly fine to sell on a publisher site.

3. Your business model allows you to choose something more effective.

Sometimes, the nature of your business allows you to move into different models.

Take, for example, the many sites that sell airline tickets. Such sites often choose an online store formula, treating seats, cars, and hotel rooms as products.

Upstart Hipmunk chose to differentiate based on the uniqueness and simplicity of their service (see Figure 3.3). They embrace the online service model. Their primary goal is to get visitors to try their innovative airline and hotel search services above all else.

Moving Beyond Pages

Clearly, your success is going to depend on a lot more than just your web pages. In the next chapter, I'll teach you specific conversion strategies for each of the five formulas. No matter which formula you use, you'll learn how to increase your conversion rates to bring in more sales for your business.

Chapter 4
Conversion is About More Than Web Pages

Conversion is about providing the right information in the right format at the right time. An irrelevant page will never convert, no matter how much you optimize it.

Most of the advice you receive about conversion centers on page optimization—testing, analytics, and best practices. Most of this advice is excellent. But, for optimization to work you must have the right pages in place, and those pages must be tied to your prospects' and customers' needs before optimization will make any difference.

The strategies I outline in this chapter take into account content, format, and continuity of your conversations with prospects. You may find yourself resisting some of these. Email may sound difficult. Social media may seem mysterious. Landing pages may feel too limiting.

Rest assured that I will outline methods to automate and shortcut the implementation of these strategies and the tactics that are their offspring.

These strategies are organized around the conversion stack, a construct that you may recognize as a sales *funnel* (see Figure 4.1).

While the sales funnel generally assumes a linear progression from awareness through consideration to action, the reality of the web is that visitors will enter and exit our influence at will.

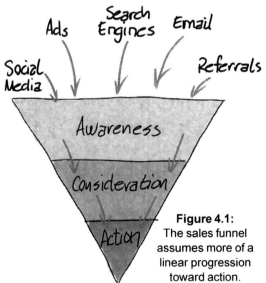

Figure 4.1: The sales funnel assumes more of a linear progression toward action.

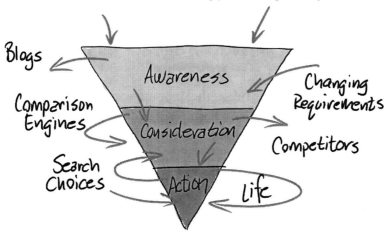

Figure 4.2: The conversion stack assumes visitors will come in and out of our influence at many points along the way.

The conversion stack (Figure 4.2) further acknowledges that when a visitor or prospect leaves our influence, other forces are acting on him, potentially diverting him from taking action.

As a result, you should be very possessive about your visitors. If they make it to your site, your first order of business is to start a conversation with them. If you can get them on the phone, great. If you can get an email address, that'll work. Perhaps they will join your social network and you can continue the conversation there.

These are the micro-conversions that lead to sales. It isn't enough to get a lead. You have to follow new leads out into their world—a world of noise, conflicting messages, misinformation, and apathy.

This realization should make you more diligent as you develop your site. It costs you something to get people to visit. Don't let go of them easily.

Conversion to Awareness, Consideration, and Action

This is a very simple model. Simple is good in the conversion game.

There are three primary conversions that must take place:

1. Conversion to awareness, in which someone becomes aware of your business and the types of problems you solve.

2. Conversion to consideration occurs when a visitor begins to consider whether or not your business can solve her problem.

3. Conversion to action happens when a prospect chooses your solution and purchases your product or service.

In the strategies I outline below, I try to include at least one for each of these conversions. Many will include getting micro-conversions that will help you maintain a conversation, identify qualified leads, and shape the kind of communication you will have with them.

Strategies for the Brochure

The brochure site is designed to appeal to those visitors who already know something about your business. Brochure sites can run the gamut: travel agencies, restaurants, dry cleaners, service contractors, and more.

Strategy 1: The Design and Layout

By "design and layout," I mean the look and feel, the colors, organization of elements, fonts, logos, and icons that inhabit the pages. Because a brochure is "safe," it is the most beholden to its design. The design takes precedent because the primary goal of the brochure is to make the business look professional, credible, and trustworthy.

It may seem ironic that this is the only formula for which I list design as a key conversion strategy. All sites need to look credible and trustworthy and support the company's brand, right?

The difference is that for the other formulas, design and layout are *supportive* of the strategies I present. For a brochure site, design and layout are *fundamental*. The other sites may get away with a poor design, but a brochure site won't.

Strategy 2: Articulate the Value Proposition

If you look around the web at brochure sites (and they are easy to find), you may be struck by the difficulty businesses have defining who they are and why they are a good choice.

This is one of the most important components of every website, but especially so for brochure sites. It is particularly important for businesses that don't have an established brand in their marketplace.

It's critical that you demonstrate value quickly and position yourself relative to your competition. It's also very difficult. This is particularly challenging for those working in the business. Marketing speakers and authors Bryan and Jeffrey Eisenberg are fond of saying, "You can't read the label from inside the bottle." It is hard to look at your own business objectively, so it helps to look at it through the eyes of your prospects and customers.

A value proposition is not a slogan. Your mission statement is most likely not an effective value proposition to your visitors.

The techniques for overcoming the barriers to developing a strong value proposition are outside the scope of this book, but you'll find Chapter 12, *Advanced Curriculum in Visitor Studies,* very helpful.

I recommend hiring a seasoned copywriter for the task—someone "outside the bottle"—and trust him to write a compelling and relevant value proposition for your site and business, no matter which conversion formula you settle on.

Strategy 3: Make it Easy to Find and Contact You

As a sales support site, the main job of the brochure is to make it easy for a prospect to find and contact the business. A conversion for a brochure site is a call, a store visit, or a completed contact form. It is important to provide as many ways to contact you as your audience will use.

Some visitors will hesitate to call, but will complete a form online. Online chat also is proving to be an important channel for many visitors.

It certainly makes sense to put contact information on the home page, and on every page, in an obvious place. Ideally, this would be above the "fold."

For businesses with multiple stores, a well-crafted "Find a store near you" page will be essential. *Warning:* If you implement something like a store finder on your site, you may want to look more closely at the online service formula.

Most of these actions can be measured in your digital lab, and monitoring "Contact Us" form completions and phone calls will tell you how your site is performing in terms of getting prospects in touch with your sales team.

> ## Important Trends for Local Businesses
>
> Brochure sites are a connector between those looking for your services and your physical locations. Today, most of your new visitors are going to come from search engines such as Google and Bing.
>
> In addition, more prospects are searching for local businesses on their mobile devices (smartphones, tablets, and GPS systems). Your *findability* will start with the search engines.
>
> Thus it is critical that you establish your place on the search engines using local Search Engine Optimization (SEO). This is a powerful technique that gives local businesses a leg up on their competition, ranking your business at the top of search results pages.
>
> Invest in making sure that those prospects driving around looking for your services find you—and not just your competitors.

Strategies for the Publication

If you're using the publication formula, I assume you're generating content—original, curated, or collected.

The primary goals of a publication site are to entice visitors to subscribe and to get them to return. Both of these goals are important whether you're selling the content or selling advertising *around* the content.

Advertisers look for eyeballs, and return visitors are key to keeping your pageviews high. Subscribers won't renew unless they are gaining value from your content that makes it worth the subscription price.

Strategy 1: Make it Easy to Find the Content

It's important that your content be organized intuitively for both new and returning visitors. By "intuitively" I mean your visitor's intuition—not yours. Your content may be well organized in your opinion, but *findability* is a more important measure of success.

The key features of findability are navigation, categories, and site search.

Navigation is crucial and should define the key categories that your visitors are looking for. Navigation cues like "Products," "Solutions," "About," and "Contact Us" are often not reflective of the visitor's frame of mind.

It is the visitor's frame of mind that counts.

What is it that brought the visitor to the site at this point in his life? Did he just get diagnosed with a leaky heart valve? Is he building his first bookshelf? Is he building his 100th bookshelf? Did he sign up for a triathlon? Does he just want to be entertained for a moment or two?

Understanding your visitors' triggers is your golden key, as this knowledge changes the types of navigation and categories you'll select.

If you want to appeal to the bored worker who only has a few minutes, you'll offer categories like "What's Hot," "Breaking News," or "Most Popular." These categories help her decide where to click.

If you want to appeal to a methodical visitor who is researching an issue, you'll want a functional or problem-oriented navigation structure.

Site search is crucial to those visitors who know exactly what they're looking for. Furthermore, your results pages must contain enough detail to help them find the content they seek. A well-designed results page is critical to successful site search.

Every audience is different. When selecting categories and navigation, do what your visitors expect, not what makes sense to you.

Strategy 2: Get Your Content Out There

Even if you don't sell subscriptions you will want subscribers. Your content provides the value of your site and is the honey that draws visitors back.

Email and social media.

Content is a terrific tool for bringing traffic to your site through email and social media. By definition, you have content to share— content that you can use to tease prospects and give them a taste of what you have to offer. Email and social media are the plates on which you serve your delicious samplings.

You can easily share whatever you're publishing across these two channels. Plus, you can track which links are generating the most visits to your site, and which are generating new subscriptions and sales.

We'll show you how to track email and social media visits in later chapters. We'll also talk about how to automate these processes so that your social networks and email "friends" are aware of what you offer.

I will argue that your primary goal is to build an email subscriber list of individuals interested in your content. Your secondary goal is to build your social networks of friends and followers who, with increasing numbers, will carry your content outward to interested and qualified prospects among their own connections.

To implement the strategy of sharing, you must embrace two key principles:

1. That your content is format independent
2. That giving away content increases the perceived value of all that you offer.

Your video content can be summarized in words and shared on social networks. You can review your eBook to create a tantalizing article on your blog. You can extract the most interesting graphs from a report to create a compelling infographic for Pinterest.

In short, the ability to mold your content for different channels means that it is easy to share, and these tastes of content will bring buyers to the doorstep of your publication site over and over again.

Strategy 3: Make it Easy to Subscribe

The process of presenting an attractive offer to your prospective buyers, making it clear to them how to take action, and then getting them through the purchase process requires your utmost attention and care.

The process is fraught with abandonment. Isn't it a shame to work so hard on your site and content, only to have the subscription process confound those who are ready to subscribe?

As you will see in later chapters, businesses assume too much when designing their subscription or registration processes. In addition, they often ignore or are oblivious to the fact that buying has emotional aspects for visitors.

Be attuned to the fact that even the simple process of asking for a name and email address can be tricky. Tread carefully here.

Strategies for the Online Store

It's hard to believe, but sales conversion rates for ecommerce sites average between two to three percent for the web as a whole. Then you have the top converting sites that convert at an estimated 15 to 20 percent or higher.

What is the difference between these high-converting sites and the rest of us? Most of these sites enjoy great brand recognition and this translates into buyer trust. Your business may not have this same level of name recognition, so you have to work harder to build trust with your visitors.

These businesses also focus on getting existing visitors to come back and buy. Visitors who have been to your site before, or who have purchased from you in the past, are far more likely to buy than "cold" strangers finding you for the first time.

High-converting businesses know this and work hard to get previous visitors and past buyers back to the site.

Strategy 1: Make it Easy to Find a Product

As with the publication formula, it is important for the online store to help the visitor find a product or, more specifically, to help her find a solution to a problem.

Whether your site is selling a catalog of products or a single item, shortening the time between a visitor's arrival and her discovery of a product she wants is a key to driving conversions and sales.

In Chapter 12, *Advanced Curriculum in Visitor Studies,* I discuss "modes of research." These include the shopper who logically explores the site to see if you have a solution to her problem. You may also be visited by the shopper who wants to take action, and will do so the moment he finds a solution that matches his desire. Be prepared to craft conversion scenarios that anticipate the ways these very different shoppers want to shop.

Strategy 2: The Product Page is Your Landing Page

A landing page is a specialized page with two primary goals:

1. Fulfill a promise made to a visitor
2. Call that visitor to take action.

Suppose a shopper clicks on a particular style of shoe on your site. The implied promise is that she will learn everything relevant about that specific shoe. The site that instead offers a list of all the shoes available breaks the implied promise.

Only a *product page* for that particular item fulfills the promise by presenting the information that the shopper needs and by offering a clear call to action such as "Add to Cart."

Furthermore, a properly optimized site will lead search engines to bring visitors directly to product pages, especially those visitors who know what they are looking for. Your product pages have to deliver the goods if you're going to get the sale.

Simplicity, relevance, and completeness are the hallmarks of a high-performing product page.

Strategy 3: Make it Easy to Buy

Unfortunately, most shopping carts are designed by engineers, who see the purchase process as a functional problem of collecting information from the visitor to process the order efficiently. Efficiency may be important to a certain segment of your buyers, but most of your buyers have very different concerns in mind as they go through the checkout process:

"Am I paying a fair price?"

"Can I trust this vendor with my credit card number?"

"What if I'm not happy with the purchase when I receive it?"

"Will shipping charges wipe away my savings?"

"Should I think about this some more before I take action?"

These are the questions that cause buyers to abandon the purchase. These are the questions that shopping carts so often fail to address. These are the questions that, if not addressed, will cost your business sales day after day.

Retrieve your shopping cart from the clutches of engineers. Put it in the hands of your visitors.

Strategies for the Consultative Site

The consultative formula is used for consultative sales, long sales cycles, or sales that involve multiple decision-makers and influencers. Businesses that sell to other businesses often face all of these obstacles.

When a consumer buys from an online store, the cost of making a bad decision is the loss of his money. In a business setting, the cost of a bad decision has implications for the buyer's career. Thus, business buyers tend to make decisions more conservatively than do consumers.

This doesn't mean that we have to treat our business visitors as logical robots. In fact, we need to take the opposite approach. Business people are still people.

The consultative formula assumes that the prospect has two primary problems:

1. Understanding the set of solutions that can be brought to bear on a complex business problem
2. Selling their recommended solution internally to influencers, gatekeepers, and check-writers.

If your website helps the prospect solve these two problems, you will be top of mind when he goes to choose vendors. This is just as important as selling him on the details of your particular solution.

Accomplishing this requires changing the purpose of your site. **For a consultative site, you cannot talk only about your company and its products. You must talk about how your visitors can solve their problems and the problems of the stakeholders they report to.**

Once you've made this fundamental shift in your thinking, you will see the folly of the business brochure as a solution for the consultative sell.

The primary strategies for the consultative site revolve around opening a channel and educating your prospects on how best to solve their problems.

Strategy 1: Help Visitors Understand their Problem

Properly implemented for conversion, a consultative site bears a striking resemblance to a publication site.

At the top of the conversion stack, a visitor is coming with a problem in mind, such as, "Employees are dissatisfied because it's too hard to manage their benefits." Her first question may be, "How are other businesses solving this problem?" Her next questions may be, "How are others in my industry solving this?" and "How are others in our state solving this?"

The consultative site tells her.

She is not yet interested in questions such as, "How will benefits management software increase employee satisfaction?" It's too soon.

If you sell such software, your site needs to talk about more than just your solution to the problem. You must consider offering your visitor:

- White papers on alternative solutions (yes, you should discuss the pros and cons of competing strategies)
- Case studies about how companies like hers solved their problems
- Articles that drill-down on specific issues
- Webinars in which she can hear other people asking the same types of questions that she has
- Blog posts by experts she can trust
- Executive summaries of key issues to share with others on her team.

None of these are provided altruistically. They are all designed to position your company as the thought leader in the space —the preferred source for answers to the visitor's problems.

When the visitor moves into questions like, "Who should I consider for benefits management software?" your solution should be top of mind. (NOTE: The visitor should move to this question much sooner if the site has educated her on the issues effectively. These strategies all involve targeted content.)

Strategy 2: Get Them to "Buy" Something with Their Contact Info

How do you stay in front of a prospect over the weeks and months it takes to make a decision?

You can do a good job of search engine optimization, and hope that he finds his way back at crucial decision points. This is too passive for a Conversion Scientist.

You can educate him through your social network, hoping he will stumble upon your content. This requires that he use social networks in his business life and that he connects with you there.

You can continue to educate him by email, sharing more of the fantastic content you've created. I think he would appreciate that, but it requires that you get an email address.

You can have your sales team call him on a regular basis to answer questions. This requires his phone number, and is very expensive.

All of these solutions are valid. The last three—social media, email, and phone contact—require the prospect to take action on your site. On a consultative site, this is considered a valuable conversion.

So, what is the prospect going to buy with his "like," his email address, or his phone number? He is buying answers—answers to the same types of questions highlighted in Strategy 1 above.

A powerful way to build a qualified house list or social network is to provide information *relevant to your prospect's problem* in exchange for his contact information or connection.

Visitors will provide contact information for almost any kind of content: webinars, reports, case studies, videos, blog post alerts, and even consultative calls from your sales team.

The key tool in all of these situations is the landing page. It may be helpful to see yourself as a content company selling reports, white papers, and consultations. Each of these very helpful items should have its own page, and that page should follow the pattern of a good landing page.

The better your landing pages, the more conversions you'll get, and the better our next strategy will work.

Prospects will generally *not* share their email address for information about your products or your company until they are well along in the decision-making process. If your competition has done the educating, they will be top of mind, not you.

Strategy 3: Use Email to Support Them in Their Decision

Like the publication site, subscribers are the lifeblood of the consultative site. In a business setting, we call them leads, but it may be more helpful to call them "students" or "information customers."

When a visitor provides her contact information, she is officially starting a conversation with your business, and you are *obligated* to carry your end of the conversation. **Anything less is a broken promise.**

Email is our tool of choice because business executives live in their email inboxes. It is how they organize their days. Email is so important that they set an alarm to tell them when new messages have arrived, allowing themselves to be interrupted by their email stream several times per hour.

Figure 4.3: IBM's Smarter Planet site uses free content to draw in visitors and "sells" higher value content in exchange for contact information.

They may not read everything you send them, but they will have to deal with everything you send. Make it good and you'll keep their trust.

These three strategies work together to position your consultative site at the center of your prospect's decision-making process. You can see this at work in the world's largest business services companies such as IBM (see Figure 4.3) and McKinsey, as well as in smaller businesses such as Trillion.

Few consulting businesses do this well, and this is an opportunity for you to outperform your competition.

Strategies for the Online Service

Like publication sites, those that sell online services have a clear advantage: Prospects can sample the service right there on the site before they buy.

The next step is to get them to actually use the service, and in the process, to convert as many of them into buyers and users as we can.

Strategy 1: Turn Visitors into Triers

It is a real advantage when a prospect can touch and feel a product. This is a major disadvantage with most products sold on the web. Not so for the online service.

With this formula, your first conversion should be a trial. You want to convert visitors into *triers.*

The key component in your visitor-to-trier conversion is your home page. I bet you thought I was going to say landing page, didn't you?

Well here's the rub. Your home page has to be designed like a landing page. In other words, the home page has to make a case for the service, make an offer, and get the visitor to take action. You'll learn more about how to do this in Chapter 10, *Getting Visitors Past the Home Page.*

Strategy 2: Use Email to Turn Triers into Buyers

Having found a trier, we now know that no matter how important our service is to her, she will not come and play with it without some prompting.

Once again, we must rely on email to keep us in the trier's mind. And one confirmation email is not enough.

As a consummate consumer of online services, I've signed up for hundreds. I'm astounded at how little email I receive from these services. More than once have I tried to sign up for a "new" service only to find out that my email address was already in use. I'd created an account in the past and had forgotten about it.

Don't be shy about helping your triers help themselves.

Here are the things you must communicate to turn triers into buyers.

Remind them of what you do.

Sure they signed up, but they'll forget what your service does. I still get email from services that I signed up for months ago—services with names like Grouply, Pageonce, Bearhug, Beetling, and Outright. Am I supposed to remember what they do from their names?

Remind them of why the service is valuable.

It isn't enough to describe your service. Remind them of the benefits that made them interested in your service in the first place. It may only take a sentence or two, but it's worth the space.

Give them a specific task.

One of my mantras is that "specificity is a hallmark of conversion." In the spirit of this, it makes sense to offer something specific to your triers. Most obvious is help using the system. Offer a video tutorial, a step-by-step explanation, or both.

If you can, suggest they complete a simple task, something that will give them a quick "win."

Ask them to become a customer.

You'll want to experiment with how often to ask a trier to become a customer, but don't make the mistake of not asking. Quickly pitch them additional features and ask them to upgrade more than once.

If you adopt a "cancel at any time" type of trial, in which a credit card is taken at the start of the trial, offer the person a way to opt-out with each email. This may sound counterintuitive, but it signals that you're not trying to take the person's money indiscriminately. It also will reduce the number of customers who call you to get a refund after their card has been charged.

Send frequently.

Don't be shy about sending these types of emails frequently. If one in three is read, you'd better send more than two. It is not spammy to send seven emails in seven days provided you are working to help people use your service for their benefit.

Leverage your deadlines.

For timed trials, you should let them know when they are approaching the end of the trial period. There is nothing like a deadline to motivate certain individuals.

A well thought-out, progressive, and helpful series of emails will not be seen as spam, and will have a positive impact on your conversions.

Strategy 3: Get Them to Login

The final conversion in an online service formula is turning customers into repeat customers. The predictive metric for renewals is *login rates*. This is the number of logins each month divided by the number of paying customers. You also may want to track your trial login rate, which is trial-account login divided by active trial customers.

Most online services offer monthly subscriptions, with discounts for those who commit to longer periods of time. Aside from delivering a great service, high-performing sites work hard to overcome the barriers to maximize renewal conversions.

Help them become experts in the use of the site.

High-converting sites become publishers of how-to videos, webinars, and blogs. AWeber, an email service provider, has an excellent blog on best practices in email marketing. They publish content that makes their customers more successful. Helping your customers is a great way to ensure they will renew their subscription month after month.

Create reasons to send email.

I was impressed by the Mint.com service, which helps its members manage their finances. The company grew its membership quickly and was bought by Intuit for $170 million just two years after its launch.

Here's a hint why. I received the email in Figure 4.4. The subject line said, "Your Money Misses You." The short email offered not one, but three links back to the Mint.com site. What triggered this email? I hadn't logged in for 30 days.

Your service probably generates daily, weekly, or monthly reasons to send a little note to your customers. You just need to think of them. Don't wait for new feature releases to talk to your users. That may be too long.

Figure 4.4: Mint.com finds ways to send its members email to get them back to the site.

And don't let your engineering team write the emails. Notice how well-crafted the Mint.com email is, reminding me of their value and teasing new features. **Every communication needs to be in the voice of the company, not the voice of an overworked developer.**

Mixing and Matching Formulas

Obviously, every business is unique. There are good reasons to choose strategies from the other conversion formulas when you're formulating your online plan.

There are bad reasons as well. Don't discard email and replace it with something else because you think email is difficult. Don't invest in expensive design services like the brochure site just because you want the site to look "better."

Remember: In the conversion game, your opinion doesn't matter—only the opinions of your best visitors should come into play. Often, you won't like what they like.

The choice is simple: Listen to your wallet or listen to your ego. Your accountant will know better than your designer whether your site is performing.

Chapter 5
Catching Conversions

Did you notice something about the strategies we discussed in the previous chapter? Each is designed to create a measureable event—to generate an action on the part of a suspect, visitor, prospect, or customer. Each strategy and tactic is designed to move a prospect through the online sales funnel like the one I showed you in Figure 4.1 on page 45.

In short, the strategies are designed to support your own conversion funnel—one that is unique to your business, and measureable through your digital lab.

In this chapter, you'll learn how to set some tripwires in your online marketing processes that will tell you when someone has moved along in the conversion process. It's like the saying, "Every time a bell rings an angel gets its wings" from the movie *It's a Wonderful Life*. We'll find those things your visitors do to ring a bell to let you know they're taking action.

Funnels Help You Generate Hypotheses

While we love to focus on that final conversion—when a visitor takes action and becomes a paying customer—many of the strategies we discussed in the previous chapter are designed to move prospects *closer* to taking action. These are "top of funnel" strategies focused on making more people *aware* of your business and dedicated to discovering prospects who are *considering* a solution like yours.

Awareness, consideration, and action—we need to see how our online marketing is performing for each of these parts of the conversion funnel. Here's why.

At the end of each month, when you sit down with the team to review the performance of your online business, you will inevitably discover that your sales are the same as the previous month, have increased, or have decreased. Your next question should be, "Why?"

If you have properly measured the journey of your customers (from total strangers to buyers), you can begin to answer that question, and to develop hypotheses as to how your online marketing affected your bottom-line results. If your sales are flat or decreasing, those hypotheses might look something like these:

"Our content hasn't been interesting to the social networks."

"Our emails aren't getting delivered."

"Our competitors have started doing something different."

"Visitors aren't finding our new products."

These kinds of hypotheses are far more powerful than the most common and more costly mantra, "We need more traffic!"

I am going to show you how to *instrument* the various funnels used in the site conversion formulas, providing you with strategies to measure the success of your online marketing from awareness through action.

Tripwires Tell You When Someone Converts

Let's start at the bottom of the funnel: action. Forms play an important part of most online conversions. Forms are used on the "Contact Us" page of the brochure site, to subscribe new members on publication sites, and to capture leads on consultative sites. They are used by online services to snag triers and by online stores to serve buyers.

In almost every case, these forms deliver a "Thank You" page or "Receipt" page once the form is successfully completed and submitted. These *confirmation* pages act as a tripwire, telling you that a visitor has passed through. Since these pages are only served up when a form is successfully completed, you know that visitors to these pages have converted.

You can track these pages in your digital conversion lab. Your analytics service holds the key. Because analytics track every page that someone visits, you can look at how many times a "Thank You" page is visited. Google Analytics goes so far as to let you set goals on these tripwire pages, and will automatically calculate your conversion rate for you.

Each Form Has its Own Conversion Rate

Since analytics also track how many visitors we are getting to any form page, we can calculate the conversion rate for individual forms.

Figure 5.1: The form conversion rate.

Not everyone is going to finish the form on our "Contact Us," "Subscribe," or "Checkout" page. To calculate the conversion rate of a specific form, divide the visits to your "Thank You" page—those who finished the form—by the number of people who visit the page with your form on it.

We'll look at ways to increase your conversion rates in Chapter 8.

Each Form Has its Own Abandonment Rate

The abandonment rate can be thought of as the inverse of the conversion rate. It measures how many people came to your "Contact Us," "Subscribe," or "Checkout" page only to navigate away without completing the process.

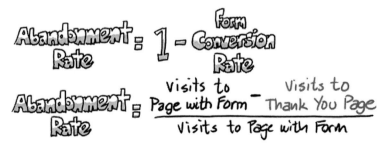

Figure 5.2: Calculating the abandonment rate of your forms.

Abandonment rates are most interesting when you have multi-step signup processes, such as the online store's checkout process. Instinctively, you will want your abandonment to be low. The lower the abandonment rate, the more people are completing the form, or the higher your conversion rate is.

Tracking Multi-Step Forms

The good news is that you don't have to collect all of this page-by-page visit information in order to calculate your conversion and abandonment rates. It is not uncommon for these processes to have multiple steps spanning two or more pages, and Google Analytics gives you the ability to define multi-step "funnels" to track them. If set up properly, you will be able to see how many visitors abandon your process at each step of the process. This tells you which pages are confounding them and which are doing a good job of getting them to take the next step.

Don't Redirect to the Home Page

It is possible that your web developer designed your forms to redirect visitors to your home page after they complete a form. This is not going to give you the information you need to track conversions in the lab. You cannot easily use the home page as a tripwire.

Insist that a special confirmation page be created for all form submissions, subscriptions, and checkout processes. In addition to being tripwires, these pages are great places to ask the customer to share on social media. They're also an ideal place to offer additional content and products for consideration. The best time to sell someone something is just after they have bought.

Tracking Subscribers to Your Email Lists

In Chapter 7, *Charge Your Marketing Batteries for More Sales,* I'll introduce you to the power of email. Email list building is a core strategy for the publication, the consultative site, and the online service. It is a natural addition to many online stores as well.

Email lists are typically built by adding a form to your site asking for, at least, a visitor's email. However, the journey of an email subscriber is fraught with peril, and subscribers can be lost at multiple points along the way. The dangers lie in visitors being sent to your email service provider's (ESP's) site to confirm their information; in the need for a confirmation email to be clicked on; and if subscribing to your site requires multiple visits. All of these factors make tracking email subscription conversion rates difficult.

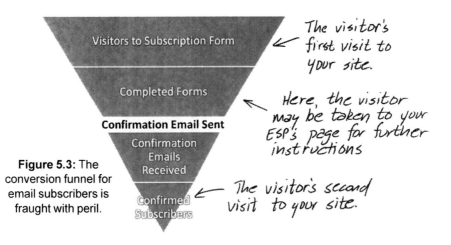

Figure 5.3: The conversion funnel for email subscribers is fraught with peril.

When you use a third-party email service provider (ESP), which I recommend, visitors may be taken to a page on the ESP's server after they submit their name and email address. To your analytics, it looks like the visitor left your site. They didn't leave. In fact, they converted. So, this creates a black hole in your analytics—a very important blind spot, because you can't easily calculate your email subscription form's conversion rate.

To complicate things further, most ESPs require a double-opt-in permission strategy. This requires that an email be sent to the prospective subscriber after they complete the form on your site. They must click on a link in that email to confirm that they did indeed want to subscribe. This requires a two-visit process. You won't know your email subscriber conversion rate unless you track visitors across these visits.

Not everyone who completes a form will confirm their subscription. Often, these confirmation emails get lost in spam filters, fail to remind the recipient why they subscribed, or are simply ignored by busy people.

For publications and consultative sites in particular, it is critical that you know your email subscriber rates. Select an ESP that lets you use your own confirmation and "Thank You" pages. These tripwires let you calculate both your form completion and your "subscription confirmed" conversion rates.

If your ESP doesn't offer the option of using your own tripwire pages, Google Analytics provides ways to track form submissions, even if they lead away from your site. This will require some simple development work. Ask your team to read up on the "Virtual URL" and "Event" features for tracking outbound clicks.

Another alternative is to use a *marketing automation service*. These services are ESPs that focus on online businesses. They can track subscribers across multiple visits, and do much more to help marketers increase conversion rates. HubSpot is an example of a service that can help with many of the strategies found in this book.

Tracking Third-Party Services

An ESP is a very helpful service, providing many of the metrics you'll want to watch from your conversion lab. However, as we just discussed, the ESP introduces some challenges in calculating conversion rates.

Anytime a third-party service is involved, it creates a discontinuity between when a visitor starts a conversion process and when he officially finishes it. It makes calculating your conversion rates a little tougher.

For example, third-party webinar services like GotoWebinar and WebEx bring your visitors to their site to sign them up for your webinars. The same is true for third-party ticketing services like EventBrite. These services make life much easier for marketers, but can challenge the Conversion Scientist in all of us. How many visitors went to their registration page but abandoned the process? In general, they can't tell you.

Ask your service providers how they can support your analytics needs. Some may integrate directly with Google Analytics. Others may give you the option of using your own tripwire pages.

Your conversion rates measure the heartbeat of your business and you should take the extra steps necessary to get the data you need.

Tracking Clicks on Content

If you're running a publication or consultative site, sharing your content with your email list and social networks is a core strategy. It is the most effective way to get prospects back to your site for another chance to convert them into a lead, customer, or subscriber.

Your ESP should provide statistics that tell you which links in your email get clicked. Further on, I'll explain the use of homing beacons to track clicks from your emails that lead back to your site so you can identify content that delivers sales and subscribers.

The Email Conversion Funnel

The journey from send to sale involves several steps. You can monitor these from your conversion lab to learn how to become a better social networker and emailer.

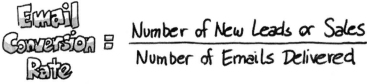

Figure 5.4: The email conversion rate.

Pay attention to the language used on the bottom of the fraction in Figure 5.4, "Number of Emails Delivered." Your ESP will calculate a *delivery* rate based on the number of emails that don't make it to their source, either because they bounced—which indicated that an email address has changed—or that they got caught in a spam filter somewhere along the way.

There are additional steps between when an email is delivered and when a prospect converts into a lead or sale.

First the visitor must *open* her email. This is tracked by your ESP and is called the *open rate.* Don't be disappointed to see that your open rate is less than 25 percent. The open rate is flawed because of the way it is measured.

A coded image is attached to your emails. When this image is downloaded from your ESP's server, it tells them that the email has been opened. Anyone who views your email with images turned off will not download any images, and will not be counted as an open. You cannot measure the open rate of text emails at all.

Here, we don't care so much about the actual percentage as much as the *change* in the percentage from email to email. If open rates go up, we can guess that the subject line or content of the email is being met with approval by our list members. A drop indicates the opposite.

Before she converts, the visitor must then *read* her email. We can't measure this in our conversion lab. What we *can* measure is the number of people who *click* on a link in the email. We call this the *click-through rate.*

The click-through rate is only *predictive* of good things. Ultimately, it will be the page to which you send them that will finally determine your *email conversion rate.* It is this page that must cajole our visitor into subscribing, buying, or filling out the form for that valuable report.

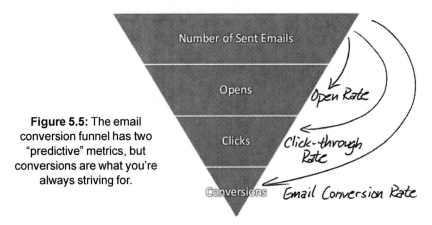

Figure 5.5: The email conversion funnel has two "predictive" metrics, but conversions are what you're always striving for.

We'll talk more about the importance of email landing pages in upcoming chapters.

When we understand the conversion rate of each email we send, it becomes much easier to decide what subject lines, content, and landing pages are going to deliver new leads, sales, and subscribers. We'll want to do more of the things that delivered that high conversion rate.

Every email is a test.

Unsubscribes: Not Necessarily Bad
There is one more thing we must watch as we send emails to our lists: the unsubscribe rate.

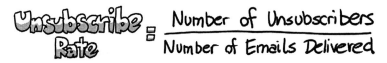

Figure 5.6: The email unsubscribe rate.

This is another metric reported by your ESP. It may sound like a terrible thing to have people unsubscribe. A high unsubscribe rate, say two percent or greater, may indicate that your email wasn't relevant to your list. It can mean that you're being too promotional.

Just as often, it means that subscribers who will never buy have dropped off your list. Just let them go. In fact, it's good practice to remove inactive names from your list, even though that's a difficult thing for most marketers to do.

Tracking Social Media Success

If you understand which content generates the most conversions, you can craft your content strategy to favor high-converting articles, blog posts, eBooks, reports, and videos. This is why you need to track visits that come from your email and social sharing.

To accomplish this, you can add **homing beacons** to your emails and social media posts. These beacons are digital capsules of information that are activated when someone clicks on one of your links. They are capable of telling you when the link was sent out, what the content was, how it was sent (e.g., by email, social post, etc.), and which service delivered it (e.g., Facebook, Twitter, ESP).

All of this gets rolled up into one (or more) Google Analytics report that tells you which social networks are generating the most subscribers and sales, which stories are clicked on the most, and how your content marketing is performing compared to search visitors, referrals, and those who click on your ads.

The technique used to attach a homing beacon to a link is called *link tagging*. It involves adding some extra text to your links—text that is recognized by Google Analytics. While it is easy to implement, it requires discipline and consistent action.

Google provides a tool that adds this special text to your links at http://support.google.com. Add this link to your conversion laboratory. (You'll also find it easier to create and track links if you download the Conversion Scientist's Link Tagging Spreadsheet.)

Scan here to download the Conversion Scientist's Link Tagging Spreadsheet.

URLs get long and look pretty ugly with the extra tags attached. I recommend dropping them into a URL shortening service such as Bit.ly or 44Doors.com/capture. These services also give you another set of analytics to track clicks on your content.

This technique can be used for any link that goes to a site that has Google Analytics installed. In fact, I tagged the QR codes used in this book so that I will be able to measure the number of direct visits this book generates.

Tracking Ecommerce Transactions

There are lots of metrics to look at in your conversion lab. Some are provided by ESPs and some are tracked by your analytics package.

However, for an online store, online service, or a publication selling subscriptions, there is one magical metric to be tracked: the sound of the cash register ringing, the completion of a transaction online.

This transactional data is most often found in your accounting databases or is kept by the merchant service that processes your credit cards. This poses a problem. If the data isn't connected to your conversion lab, it is hard to track revenue back to your visitors. This is a big issue, because the most important metric in any online business is the revenue generated.

You may be flattered that people are clicking through from your emails and social media posts. You may be honored that they are subscribing to your email lists. But when you know *which* emails, social media posts, ads, and search keywords are generating the most in sales, you can make business-changing decisions based on bottom-line information.

Too often we have ads and emails that generate lots of clicks, but they don't generate sales and subscriptions. This information is only *predictive*. We want to know how many people *bought* and how much they spent for each ad, email, etc. This information is *definitive*.

This is why online stores, online services, and publications selling subscriptions should add sales tracking to their conversion labs. Fortunately, Google Analytics offers a way to do this. It will take a little work from your web developer or shopping cart vendor, but it enables you to measure *revenue per visit* (RPV). This is the revenue generated by your site divided by the total number of visitors.

This helps you identify which advertising programs you should invest in. If your RPV is $2.00 and you're paying $4.00 per click through your search ads, you may be losing money on that traffic.

Tracking Transactions with Google Analytics

The only way you can generate reports that tell you which types of visitors are buying is by giving Google Analytics the details of each transaction executed on your site. Otherwise, determining which traffic source generated which purchases is very difficult. Fortunately, Google Analytics makes this relatively easy.

You'll need to engage a developer to set this up for you. He will program your receipt or "Thank You" page to send transactional information to Google Analytics, including:

- Total transaction value
- The product name for each item bought
- The price of each item bought
- The product SKU of each item bought
- The shipping cost
- Sales tax charged.

If you provide this information, Google Analytics will keep track of the source of buyers for you and deliver these fantastic reports.

You'll never make better decisions about where to spend your hard-earned marketing dollars than you will with this kind of data.

> **Google Analytics Won't Match Your Accounting System. That's Okay.**
>
> Don't be alarmed that the revenue reported by Google Analytics is different than the revenue reported by your accounting system or merchant service.
>
> Google Analytics will not reflect returns and cancellations, and there are other anomalies that will keep the two revenue numbers from balancing. As long as your Google Analytics revenue numbers *correlate with,* or follow, your internal system's numbers, you can use analytics to make decisions about your business.

Don't be Deceived by Visitors

Tripwires can tell you how many visitors turn into customers, but they can't tell you how much they spent and which items they bought.

When Google Analytics is tracking your transactions, you get some stunning reports and metrics for your conversion lab.

Campaign	Visits	Revenue ($)
Email #4	218	$2,452.27
Email #2	386	$2,138.08
Email #5	120	$1,636.76
Email #1	196	$826.46

Figure 5.7: In this report, email 2 generated many more visitors, but fewer sales, than email 4.

Figure 5.7 shows that email 4 generated more revenue than email 2, even though email 2 brought almost twice as many visits to the site. Likewise, email 1 outperformed email 5 in terms of visits, but email 1 generated only half of the revenue.

You want to be making decisions about your marketing based on the bottom line. This online store owner will not be deceived by visits and will send out more emails like email 4 and email 5.

Likewise, you'll want to measure your other efforts based on the sales generated. All of your online programs should be measured by this standard.

You only want to add names to your mailing list if your emails are generating revenue. You only want to grow your social network if your social networks are generating revenue. By tracking ecommerce data in your conversion lab, you can easily see which efforts are making money and which are not.

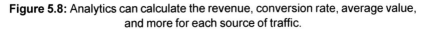

Traffic Source	Visits	Revenue	Ecommerce Conversion Rate	Transactions	Average Value	RPV
Organic	52,234	$24,740.56	0.65%	341	$72.55	$0.47
(None)	8,950	$14,663.79	2.35%	210	$69.83	$1.64
Referral	10,034	$6,036.39	0.98%	98	$61.60	$0.60
Email	754	$3,278.73	5.84%	44	$74.52	$4.35

Figure 5.8: Analytics can calculate the revenue, conversion rate, average value, and more for each source of traffic.

Figure 5.8 is a report from Google Analytics that tells us quite a bit about the marketing channels one company is investing in. This company had invested heavily in organic search engine optimization, and you can see the fruits of their labor. Most of their traffic and revenue comes from that source, and those buyers spend $72.55 per purchase on average.

You can also see that email traffic is a very valuable, though a smaller percentage of traffic. Email visitors convert to buyers at a higher rate than the other channels, and they buy more when they purchase, with an average value (or *average order value*) of $74.52.

The data tells this company that they should invest in building their email list, and should consider sending more email. The *revenue per visit* (RPV) column shows that each visit from their email campaigns puts $4.35 into this company's pocket. Organic visits earn less than 50 cents per visit, though organic visitors clearly "make it up on volume."

Without understanding these dynamics, the owners might have dismissed email as a poor revenue generator instead of acting to leverage the high conversion rates and high average order values offered by email subscribers.

Earlier we talked about the difference between low-quality traffic and highly qualified traffic. If you want a definitive measure of the quality of any traffic source, look no further than RPV. Once you know where the high-quality visitors are, you just have to figure out how to get more of them to your site.

Tracking Calls

In almost every one of these conversion formulas, it's important to offer a variety of ways for a visitor to take action. Phone calls are a natural way to buy for many customers, especially those who don't trust the web with their credit card information.

Most online stores will offer a way to buy by phone. Similarly, there is no better outcome for consultative sites than to have a prospect call to discuss their problems. Clearly, the phone is going to be an integral part of the online buying process for a long, long time.

Unfortunately, most calls that are influenced by the web are not counted in the site's conversion rate. Our analytics data may tell us that ads are not performing well. However, we may find that those who respond to our ads prefer to call, and that, when we include the phone sales, the ads are performing very well.

The reason calls are not typically included is that salespeople and call center staff are notoriously poor at tracking the source of their calls. They are incentivized to answer questions in the shortest time possible and to close sales. Asking where the caller heard about them quickly gets forgotten as they work toward their primary goals.

Answering the question, "How many callers went to the web first?" is relatively easy to do. You simply place a different phone number on the website—a number that you don't advertise anywhere else. At the end of that month, you look at your phone bill and count up the number of calls made through the web-only number.

Another alternative is to offer web-only specials to callers. The caller asks for the web special when they call, telling the salesperson that they are a web-influenced prospect. You can calculate the number of web specials sold from your accounting system.

These are not highly integrated approaches. The data we need isn't funneled into our conversion lab for analysis. It is difficult to know how many of the callers bought, and how much they bought.

Fortunately, there are analytics services focusing on callers that you can add to your conversion lab. Mongoose Metrics (MongooseMetrics.com) and If By Phone (IfByPhone.com) are two companies that track callers back to their source. They can get quite sophisticated in their tracking, assigning unique phone numbers to individual visitors. Of key importance, these services integrate with Google Analytics, which means that the data they collect can be linked in your conversion lab.

Tracking Store Visits

If you're serious about understanding how your website affects your business, and your goal is to get people into your stores, you need to understand how your website is influencing this.

Unlike call tracking, there is no magical analytics tool that will do this for you. You're going to have to resort to something like old-fashioned couponing.

By offering a coupon, you can at least get an idea of the influence the web is having on your store traffic. Coupons have a number of drawbacks though:

- Printing coupons will be seen as inconvenient by all but the most price-sensitive shoppers
- The cost of tracking the coupons you receive each day may end up being more costly than the value of the data you collect.

Providing a coupon page formatted for mobile devices will get visitors past the problem of printing coupons. Furthermore, you can look at visits to your coupon page in your analytics and use that number as a measure of potential store visits.

This is a less-than-perfect way to track store visits, but it can be very helpful to have an idea of how web traffic is turned into foot traffic.

Bring it All Together in Your Conversion Lab

We've touched on a number of ways to measure your conversion funnels in this chapter. Ultimately, you will want to consolidate as much as possible into one place. The most common tool for consolidating such a mélange of information is the spreadsheet.

Your skills with a spreadsheet are ultimately going to expand or limit your decision-making ability. You and your team should invest in and exercise your skill with rows, columns, and formulas. However, we don't want your weekly or monthly analytics review to turn into "spreadsheet hell."

If you're using Google Analytics in your lab, you will find some very good applications that can help you automatically draw information directly into a spreadsheet. Visit the Google Analytics Application Gallery (Google.com/analytics/apps) to explore some of these tools.

In the end, if your regular reporting process takes hours to complete, you will stop doing it. Busy days will cause you to delay your data gathering. Without the data, your decisions will suffer and so will your business. At some point, the cost of collecting and analyzing data will outstrip its value. Make good decisions about what you need and how hard you're willing to work to get the business insights that your conversion lab can deliver.

Chapter 6
How Content Fuels Conversion

Of the five conversion formulas—the brochure, the publication, the online store, the consultative site, and the online service—only one is called "publication." Yet, the strategies found in the other four sound suspiciously like things publishers would do:

- Produce articles, reports, and webinars (that help business buyers solve their problems) to generate leads
- Deliver content by email to prospects, subscribers, and triers
- Use content to entertain and engage your social networks.

You may not fancy yourself to be another Rupert Murdock, but **if you're going to convert, you're going to have to publish.**

Powering Your Online Marketing

In high-school chemistry class, we were provided with Bunsen burners—those little super candles that made so many of our experiments react. The flame made inert chemicals combine into more interesting things. This flame made reactions go faster, and it was one of the coolest parts of chemistry lab.

Likewise, in your digital conversion lab, you need something to make prospects react to your solution.

A Bunsen burner is fed by a little tube connected to a propane tank hidden somewhere out of site. It is the propane that puts the "burn" in the burner.

Content is the fuel of our business' online fire. Content generates light and heat, and people react to that. Like propane, content burns away. Like propane, content must be replenished and refilled.

When the fuel that feeds your flame runs out, the light that guides the world to your business flickers and dies.

If you're marketing online, you're publishing online.

The "Markishing" Department

Get ready to have some fun.

In your new markishing department (marketing/publishing takes too long to type), you're going to experiment with novel types of media, develop landing pages in unexpected places, and move from a campaign orientation to a momentum orientation.

And in the process, you're going to learn a great deal about your company, its products, and your brands by looking at yourself through your visitors' eyes.

First, you'll need to fill out your team. Then, you'll take an inventory of the types of content your audience needs and compare it to the content you already produce. Finally, you'll create a markishing machine that engages your audience on a daily or weekly basis.

The Markishing Team

I've had the privilege of working with some amazing teams of "A" players in the online marketing game. These team members are generally grouped and labeled as designers, marketers, information architects, and developers. In my experience, you're going to need to add some different birds to the aviary.

A Storyteller

There is a way of writing that is fundamentally human. The humanness of such writing should shine through in any online situation, even in the "professional speak" that so many of us seem to think business people like to read.

Case in point: Groupon. This "deal-a-day" site offers its email subscribers discounts from local businesses.

Groupon is a publication site, not an online store. They publish deals. Their lifeblood is getting subscribers onto their free email list and then keeping those subscribers interested day after day.

You'd think that discounts of 50 percent or more would be engaging enough for email content. Groupon didn't. The company sends dozens of deals a day. Nonetheless, they craft witty, entertaining, and fun descriptions for each one of the products and offers they promote.

This flies in the face of reports and research that says web surfers don't read. The truth is that web surfers don't read content that is crappy, colorless, tasteless, and irrelevant. Groupon writes these descriptions for their customers because they recognize that the businesses that pay them don't know how to write, especially about themselves.

After years of blogging, writing columns, and authoring books, I have to be close to the 10,000 hours of writing that Malcolm Gladwell claims makes me an "outlier." Nonetheless, I don't feel qualified to write persuasive copy for my clients. You shouldn't either.

Marketing people may be great at messaging and positioning. This is only half the battle. Get a good copywriter, pay them exorbitantly, and then measure the results.

Avoid copywriters who write "business speak." Business speak seems safe, but has little in the way of storytelling, metaphor, and the proper omission of detail that lets a reader's imagination take over. As if this wasn't enough, most copywriters' work is then edited by the marketing team, by one or more executives, and then vetted by the legal department, none of whom have the training to write truly persuasive copy.

By the time the copy has completed this gauntlet of red ink, any remaining color, taste, and freshness will have been wringed out until it is "squeaky clean, like a Styrofoam sandwich," to quote author Tom Robbins in his book, *Fierce Invalids Home from Hot Climates.*

Hire a talented copywriter who has been tested in the marketplace. Trust him, correcting only factual errors. Then measure the results of his work using your conversion lab. Does his writing decrease bounce rates on a page? Does it increase click-through rates for your email? Does it improve conversion rates on your landing pages?

This more than anything will increase the value of your white papers, articles, videos, social network posts, and landing pages to your prospects.

A Draftsman

Conversion Scientists rely heavily on designers to do the job of getting our strategies out onto the digital page. However, there is a natural tension between us. The reason is that we need a different kind of creativity than that instilled in most designers.

We need designers who are more like draftsmen than artists.

In the real world, a draftsman is a problem-solver, working to find the optimal routing for pipes and conduits in buildings, the best path for roads within the city, and the most efficient layout for microscopic wires in a crowded microchip.

In your digital world, you want a person on staff who is designing the optimal routes for the human eye. This person should be comfortable guiding the path of your visitors' eyes like a conductor's baton guides musicians' eyes.

If I ask a designer to make one element the most prominent item on a page, a draftsman-style designer will hear, "Surround it with white space, make it stand out on the background, choose a color that is not a part of the page's color palette, and make sure it is above the 'fold.'"

Too many creative designers are concerned about things like the "balance" of the elements on the page, the "consistency of color" and too often simply do what everyone else is doing.

Once the logo and style guide is done, keep your draftsman close. And always measure the results of his work. A good designer can easily swallow his pride to learn from real bottom-line feedback.

An Imagemaker

If words are so powerful, then why do we need images? The answer is that humans love images and pictures, especially if they tell a story.

Unfortunately, stock photos seem to rule on the Internet. It's as if designers see images as an afterthought to their logos, taglines, fonts, and color palette.

Here's a great test for your site. Go to the pages frequented by your visitors and look at the images there. Try to write a caption for each image.

First, put on your designer's hat and see if you can ferret out the reason why he chose the picture.

iStockPhoto

Figure 6.1: What does this image say to the reader?

The designer's caption for the image in Figure 6.1 might have been, "If you buy from us, pretty people like me will like you!"

I took this image from a site that should follow the consultative site formula. I call this kind of image "business porn."

Next, put on your cynical hat. What does the image really say? For the one in Figure 6.1, I might say "Hi! I'm here to appeal to the base urges of our mostly male audience."

If a picture is worth a thousand words, a bad picture is worth a thousand needles in the eye. Your imagemaker will focus on the following best practices when selecting and creating images for your site.

Show the Product

This is obvious for an online store, but less so for the other formulas.

How can a consultative site "show the product?" Remember that a consultative site is selling informational products. Render your PDF reports and eBooks to show what they would look like if they were printed and bound. Provide pictures of DVDs complete with labels to highlight your online video. There are a number of online services, desktop software, and Photoshop plugins designed to render realistic reports, books, and DVDs.

Alternatively, choose pictures of your authors or presenters for reports and webinars, especially if they have recognizable faces.

For the online service, screen shots are commonly used. However, you don't have to show the whole screen. Focus on a portion of the screen that highlights an important feature. Remember that even screen shots need to tell a story. You don't want to confuse the visitor and have them perceive that you offer a complicated service.

Create Images that Capture the Imagination

How do you "show" a special paint that reflects heat away from a home or building? You can show a big can of paint, or you can get a little creative, as Radiosity Radiant Barriers (Radiosity3000.com) did.

Figure 6.2: How do you "show" paint that reflects heat away from your home? Radiosity Radiant Barriers nails it.

Take a look at Figure 6.2. Is there any doubt that there's something special about the paint on this roof?

Every Image Should Have a Caption

Captions are one of the most read parts of a page. You should provide a caption for each image.

The caption does not have to explain the picture. In fact, this is a great place to re-state your offers. Get your ace copywriter involved, as good captions can be as important as good headlines.

Every Image Should be Clickable

People expect to be able to click on images. They want to click on relevant images even more so. If you doubt this assertion, we can prove it with a new addition to your digital lab. Install a service like CrazyEgg (CrazyEgg.com) or ClickTale (ClickTale.com). You will get a heat map of where visitors are clicking on your pages. These heat maps are very enlightening, and you'll see that images draw many clicks.

For images on the product pages in your online store, clicks could take visitors to a larger version of the image. For brochures, publications, consultative sites, and online service sites, take them to a page that includes the image, but offers more content. In other words, take them to a landing page.

More and Bigger is Better for Online Stores

The more photos you place on your online store, the better. Show the product from all angles, in high resolution. Make sure that the items are well-lit and in focus. Quality photos sell.

Show your products being used, worn by a model, or manipulated. Successful apparel retailers show their apparel with a variety of accessories to capture the visitor's imagination.

Remember that to maximize your conversion rates, you have to get the user as close to touching, tasting, and feeling your products as possible. Images offer a great way to do this.

Video Rocks Conversion

What happens when your imagemaker gets together with your storyteller and mixes in some *motion?*

Magic, according to tests I've seen involving video.

If a picture is worth a thousand words, then a video is worth 30,000 words per second. Only the most accomplished writers can convey music and motion in their writing. Writers like that can be expensive.

Video offers a way to sustain a visitors' attention, to present concepts quickly, and to get viewers' eyes, ears, and imagination all engaged at the same time.

The fear among many businesses is that video is difficult and expensive to produce, and if it is done wrong, you will have engaged all of the visitors' senses in making a fool of yourself. As it turns out, video is rather forgiving. Buyers are forgiving of production quality, and you don't have to produce commercial-quality videos to be persuasive.

A number of different types of video have proven effective in moving viewers closer to buying.

Slide Video

Some high-converting videos have been created with PowerPoint slides, screen recording software such as Camtasia (Techsmith.com/camtasia), and an inexpensive headset mic. Many businesses simply record the webinars they deliver, which are almost always driven by slide presentations.

Tip: You can add a little more motion to your video using the innovative presentation software Prezi (Prezi.com).

Motion Graphics

Motion graphics can be used to generate some amazing video without the studios, lights, and actors usually associated with video production. These videos are produced by moving words and shapes to tell your stories.

Drawn Video

You may be familiar with the popular videos of RSA Animate on YouTube. They produce whiteboard drawings over the audio of some very interesting presentations. Drawn video can be quite expensive to produce, but this style of video is proving to be absolutely captivating to visitors. These videos tend to get shared as well.

Product Videos

Online stores take note. In most cases, product videos will easily pay for the cost of video production by increasing conversion rates and average order values. According to Zappos' Rico Nasol, the apparel retailer saw increases in revenue of between six percent and 30 percent.

By the beginning of 2010, Zappos had 10 studios working full-time to get video for thousands of products on its site.

Audio Quality Matters

If there's one place to not skimp, it's on the audio. "Invest in cheap cameras and expensive mics" is the motto of the video production team that gets it done.

Search Engines Love Video

Make sure your video is available for search engines to find.

Google has implemented Universal Search, in which all kinds of media get included on their results pages: maps, images, and video. Bing and Yahoo! Search integrate these alternative media into their search results pages as well.

The thing is, video seems to be brought to the top of the search results for no other reason than it is video. **Use video to leapfrog your competitors in search, even if their content is better optimized.**

Video in the Lab

The types of product videos that will work is quite dizzying. You could produce product-only shots, products being used or worn by models, products being demonstrated by salespeople, and even user-generated testimonials.

I recommend testing several different styles and lengths of video on a selection of products. Once you can tell which one increases sales the most for your particular audience, you can roll that style out across all products.

The key to measuring video lies in the capabilities player that resides on your site and delivers the video. The YouTube player is quite common, and YouTube is providing an increasing number of analytics to tell you how much time visitors are spending with your video. However, we need to tie video to our conversion goals. We want to be able to answer the question, "How did video impact our bottom line—by delivering more leads, sales, or subscriptions?"

One way to do this is to integrate your video player with Google Analytics. Inexpensive players such as the JW Player from Longtail Video (LongTailVideo.com) provide hooks that you can use to tell Google Analytics when someone has watched a video and how far into the video they got before moving on. With one report, you can then see if the visitors who watched the video were more likely to convert than those who didn't.

A Search Engine Translator

Regardless of how good your advertising and marketing are, one thing is certain: More and more of your traffic is going to come from search engines.

The top search engines on the Internet now include Google, Bing, and YouTube, and these are influenced by social sites like Facebook and Twitter. Social networks benefit from a community that helps to sift and tag your content.

Google, Bing, and YouTube suffer from a fundamental lack of comprehension. Your site has the burden of communicating its content and value to these search engines, and it's a lot like talking to the autistic savant Raymond from the Tom Cruise movie *Rainman*. Raymond was the character who could repeat facts and do calculations with amazing precision. However, Raymond—like the search engines—could only understand the literal meaning of what he heard and read.

Google has made efforts to reward sites that have plentiful content, and prefers sites with frequently updated content. Hire an SEO specialist to ensure that your content is being found by the search engines. Your efforts will be rewarded with increased standing for your site, which will translate into more traffic.

From a conversion standpoint, look for SEO experts that have the following characteristics:

They talk about traffic, not ranking.

If they are overly focused on your ranking, proceed with caution. You can easily rank for keywords that aren't being searched, or for keywords that bring the wrong kinds of eyeballs—eyeballs that don't want what you offer.

They are picky about the pages they send traffic to.

The best SEO firms have a conversion practice. They will want to optimize pages that are designed to convert visitors.

You can optimize the home page for search all day long, but it is your product and landing pages that will convert search traffic best (as you will soon discover). That is what they are designed for. Hire a search resource that is focused on optimizing effective pages.

Original content is a key to their strategy.

The algorithms that Google and Bing use to prioritize websites like yours change once or twice a year. One strategy that seems to be consistently effective is original content.

Your search engine translator should encourage you to use original content to create keyword-rich content for your site, to place that content on other sites, and to use it in social media. These activities work to build the authority of your site.

Internal vs. External Resources

It isn't critical that your markishing team be made up of employees of your company. In fact, you'll probably find a mix of internal and external resources to be most effective.

Keep in mind that great content is more successful than mediocre content. Make sure you have the writers, designers, photographers, videographers, and other professionals that have the right skills to deliver the goods.

External resources can open production bottlenecks. An employee who is developing your content "in her spare time" may not be able to deliver with frequency when she gets busy, and momentum is important to content strategy. A whip-cracking project manager will ensure that you have a consistent stream of content for your eager audience.

Budget appropriately for content. It will pay you back.

Agility and Scale

Once you have this team of professionals in place, get the organizational inertia out of their way. Organizational inertia is defined as "the way we have always done things." It is particularly empowered by short-term thinking.

The challenge is to shift from project- or campaign-based planning to a more constant and long-term approach. You are no longer creating six-month campaigns based on one set of messaging and creative. You're creating 50 pieces of content over a year or more, each influenced by current events and the needs of your prospects.

As you should now see, **every communication is an experiment**. You can track the success of each of your digital communications down to the item and channel. Feedback is essentially instantaneous.

What you learn from the success of a blog post will influence what you write about in future posts. Heavy attendance at a webinar tells us we will do well to create an on-demand version and *cascade* that content into other media channels.

A data-driven content plan requires a specialized kind of project manager.

Borrowing from our friends using the publication formula, a *managing editor* may be needed to keep the editorial quality of your marketing relevant, on-time, and on-target. If you have a team developing an online service, you might draw from their agile development training to find a *scrum master* to provide the agile marketing mojo needed to manage short, frequent "sprints" of content development. We created an *implementation manager* role at Conversion Sciences to guide our clients in their ongoing content development and testing.

The bottom line is that you need someone who understands that content has a very important role in your online business—someone who will ask questions such as:

"Does our editorial calendar need to change based on current events?"

"Did someone look at the results of the last communication?"

"Based on past results, what should we be producing today?"

These are different questions than those asked by traditional project managers. Look for professionals who can pull this off.

Sources of Content

It is outside the scope of this book to speculate on all of the sources of content for your digital marketing strategy. It is more important that you grasp two ideas that will keep the thought of being a "publisher" from freezing you in place:

1. Every business creates content every day.
2. Digital media is flexible, moldable, and can be reshaped quite easily. Bend, fold, spindle, and mutilate at will.

So ask yourself this question: What is your business creating every day?

Sales Communication

Ultimately, your salespeople are the ones who have to explain your business to prospects. Often, they end up translating what your marketing people write into English, targeting the message at the influencers, gatekeepers, and champions they are trying to close.

Why not adopt some of this content for your site? It can be used for everything from articles to buyers' guides.

Customer Support

Gather the questions most commonly asked by customers and summarize them in a report. Many of these questions will pertain to post-purchase concerns. This is very helpful to a prospect who must look into the future to anticipate questions that won't arise until after the deal is done, when her job and reputation are on the line.

Subject Matter Experts

How does your organization learn about your products and services? They learn from the employees who are creating those products and services. Somehow, your organization teaches itself a lot.

Those communications—emails, manuals, presentation slides, video, and audio from scholarly presentations—will be helpful to your customers and potential customers as well. You just have to go out and find them, and turn them into something your visitors can consume.

Employees with Interesting Hobbies

Peter Scoble is a photographer and videographer. He also happened to work for a company called Microsoft. While there, he used his love of video and his blog to become an unofficial spokesman for the company. His interviews with Microsoft intelligentsia were shared on his blog for everyone to see. He became a very human face to a very corporate technology company.

What interesting hobbies do your employees have? I know you have writers who can contribute to a blog. Maybe you have DJs, photographers, music aficionados, or designers who enjoy creating infographics. Seek them out and give them something to do for you.

Cascading Content

Is this starting to sound like a lot of work to you? It is true that content must be found, edited, and shared on a regular basis to feed the markishing machine you're creating.

However, digital content has legs. One item of content can be cascaded into a variety of channels like a fountain of champagne glasses at a wedding.

For example, how many opportunities do your employees get to present at conferences, training sessions, seminars, and webinars? If the answer is "none," then it's easy enough to create a webinar or seminar for yourself. Film them and record good quality audio. This bubbly content fills the top glass of your cascade.

Have someone edit the video into a series of shorter videos, ripe for YouTube and other video services. You've just filled the next layer of glasses.

Share the slides used on slide-sharing services such as SlideShare (Slideshare.net) and Scribd (Scribd.com). SlideShare makes it easy to add the audio from the presentation onto the slides, giving you an on-demand presentation for your website. Voila—another, wider layer of glasses fills with sparkling champagne.

For just a few dollars, the video can be transcribed. Lay this out as a report or white paper and distribute it for lead generation. Another layer of glasses fills.

The transcript is then diced into smaller pieces for blog posts. Each blog post advertises itself in short descriptions to be shared via email and on Twitter, Facebook, LinkedIn, and other social networks. Each email and social media post brings interested customers and new prospects to the blog where they are educated or entertained—as well as introduced to your solutions and services. Each visit is also being measured by your conversion lab equipment to see what increases your conversion rates.

Soon, one event has filled the glasses for the entire wedding party and guests, tickling noses and fueling teary toasts.

The talents needed to create this content cascade are not necessarily expensive. The transformations discussed in this example are often not time-intensive. Yet, the momentum created by this unfolding of digital content provides a great way to identify the topics and issues that bring new people into your sphere of influence.

Through your conversion lab, you will learn which formats and topics make the cash register ring. Spend your money on that kind of content.

Tap the Natural Power of the Internet

Geologists can tell us something about getting attention. They deal every day with heat and light and the building blocks of our planet. They spend their time measuring the forces that shake the ground, cause violent eruptions, and move mountains. These are things no one can miss.

Geologists know what makes a volcano erupt—and when that happens, it gets everyone's attention. That's exactly what we want from our content strategy. Yes, your business can tap the natural power of the Internet much like a volcano taps forces deep within the earth.

Change Your Mind About Blogs

If you think a blog is just "social media," then you must expand your thinking.

A blog is first and foremost a content source. It is a publishing platform with a specific structure: stories are listed starting from the most recent to the oldest. This is called Last In, First Out (LIFO) in scientist lingo. Each post gets its own page, and these pages serve as landing pages for visitors. As such, they must be designed to convert interested readers.

It is the **culture of blogs** that your company can leverage to gain momentum and scale. This culture is strikingly different from the book, news, and magazine publishing culture, in which editors sift for grammatical errors, journalists strive to avoid opinion, and advertising is held at arm's length.

Blogs are held to a different standard.

Blog posts are educational and entertaining first, promotional second. You can talk about your new product on your blog, but simply posting a press release isn't going to pass the "educational and entertaining" test. You don't have to be as stuffy or "safe" on a blog as you do when writing for a brochure site.

Blog posts do not have to follow strict editorial convention. The blogosphere says, "We would rather have your imperfect content than to not have it at all." It is generally okay if there are typos and grammatical errors. You may wish to hold your brand to a higher standard, but you must balance editorial standards against achieving a higher frequency of publication.

A blog post is written by an individual. The prominence of an individual author opens the door for more editorial freedom among blog readers. Even for corporate blogs, there should be a human being listed on the byline of each post.

A blog post can contain anything. Blogs are designed to enable expression. Text, videos, pictures, infographics … all are fair game for a blog.

A blog post can drill down into minute details, or describe the sweeping landscapes of your marketplace.

How do these cultural oddities help your business' conversion rate?

- First, they allow you to discard the long writing and editing cycles that form mud around the tires of most email newsletters. Shorter cycles mean more content, more fuel for the burner.
- The personal nature of this culture means that more of the people you work with can contribute. Anyone in your company can develop a reputation in the blogosphere. From engineering to finance, you will find people with unusual knowledge about your business— knowledge that could help prospects find their way to being customers.
- Finally, you are no longer limited to the written word. Every business like yours has natural abilities. A design firm may love creating infographics. A wedding video company better be able to create some interesting videos. A hunting dog supply should be able to get a few pictures of hunting dogs in action.

All of this content works on blogs, and it is unshackled by the blogosphere's embrace of human nature. Honor your brand, but high production values are not a prerequisite for successful content.

How a Blog is Like a Volcano

At its most basic level, a volcano spews hot, molten rock out onto the surface of the earth, building a mountain as this rock collects and cools. A volcano is fueled by a magma chamber deep in its belly. The magma is rock that has been melted by heat and pressure as the continent-sized plates of the Earth's crust grind against each other.

At its most basic level, a blog spews content like a volcano spews lava. The content builds up on your blog like magma builds in a volcano's chamber.

All you need to do is tap that source and the hot rock and gases will put on a show.

How Blogs Share Themselves

Just as a volcano has many vents for hot gases and lava, your blog has many outlets to the surface of the web. The primary path for content to find the light of day is through a "syndication feed," also called an RSS feed.

You've no doubt seen the little orange icon that indicates a feed is available on a blog. This feed is a way for other computers to read your blog. Some very interesting things can be done when your content becomes available to other computers:

- Your posts can be piped into anyone's feed reader, where they are prompted to read your posts even if they haven't visited your site.
- Posts can be automatically posted on Twitter, Facebook, LinkedIn, and almost any social network through a variety of free services and apps. This exposes the friends of your business—and all of their friends—to your content.
- Feed-driven magazines, such as Flipboard, Zite, Summify, and Paper.li, deliver your content in newspaper format to subscribers who follow you on Twitter and Facebook. Mobile devices and tablets become windows into your business.
- ESPs, such as MailChimp (MailChimp.com), offer services that will deliver automatically generated newsletters to your email list when new posts appear on your blog.
- A variety of directories will take your RSS feed and publish your stories on their sites. This builds your credibility with search engines and can bring additional traffic.

As you can see, the opportunities for other computers to share and spread your blog content are numerous. We will drill down on several of these strategies in the chapters ahead.

Growing Mountains

The image of the smoking mountain, filling the horizon and commanding respect, is exactly the sort of thing your blog can deliver. The more content your blog delivers, the more visible the blog becomes. Search engines take notice. The dynamic content will naturally be rich with relevant keywords, and search engines reward this with higher placement on results pages.

A steady stream of tips, how-to's, analyses, and opinions will make the blog **rise higher in the minds of email subscribers and social media connections**, positioning your company as a leading source of solutions in your marketplace.

Finally, competitors will tread carefully along the slopes of your content, fearful that a viral eruption may burn them at any time.

Viral Eruptions

Despite their years of experience, geologists cannot predict when a volcanic eruption might occur. Likewise, we can't predict when a certain piece of content is going to capture the imagination of the population and erupt into traditional media channels. Many have tried. Those who have succeeded in having content "go viral" have generally been very surprised at their good fortune.

Likewise, your markishing team won't know when the time and the story are right for a perfect storm of free exposure. However, your business will enjoy the benefits of many smaller eruptions if you keep your magma chamber stocked with content and share it regularly.

This is how your volcano is built—one small eruption at a time.

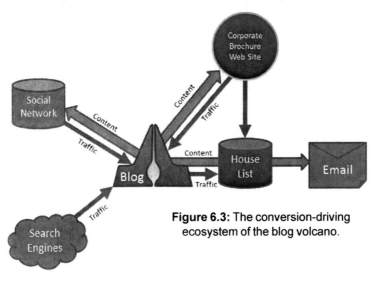

Figure 6.3: The conversion-driving ecosystem of the blog volcano.

A Complete Ecosystem

Here's how the blog volcano ecosystem gets people to your site.

Content is posted as a blog. The RSS feed has been supplied to your ESP, which is watching for the new content. Once it's there, the content is dropped into a nicely designed template and sent to your email list. Recipients interested in the story click through to read more. Your blog reminds them of who you are, what you do, and the problems that you solve.

The RSS feed has been provided to a service such as TwitterFeed (Twitterfeed.com) that will automatically send the blog title and a link to your Twitter followers. A similar service does the same for Facebook. These posts appear on your wall and in the news feeds of your fans. Those who find the content relevant click through to see the content.

The new content on your site gets the attention of the search engines, which send traffic to your site.

Every time someone clicks through to your site—from social media, search engines and email—you encourage them to subscribe to your email newsletter, to become a fan, or to follow you on Twitter. This multiplies the number of people who could see future posts when shared through these channels.

On your content pages and in your content, you will include opportunities for them to buy, to become a lead, to start a trial, or to purchase a subscription.

This is how it works. More relevant, content-driven traffic jumping into your conversion funnels—and most of the effort is automated.

Doesn't this make you look at your blog with a fresh pair of eyes?

Monitor How Your Content is Performing

As we said in the previous chapter, content is tracked by clicks and conversions. Your digital conversion lab can help you understand which content your readers love, and which content is making them yawn. Watching the clicks and conversions on specific content through each channel will help you shape your content development strategy and bring more business to your site.

Next, we'll look at how to store some of the traffic we've invested in so that we can get more from our content and advertising.

Chapter 7
Charge Your Marketing Batteries for More Sales

Your online marketing program, built from the latest in digital tools, enabled by high bandwidth connectivity and powered by every imaginable form of media, also must be charged frequently.

Your online marketing machine runs on attention, not electricity. You feed your machine with attention-creating advertisements. Each turn of the advertising crank generates the attention that brings new visitors and returning customers to your site.

However, when you don't turn the crank—when you stop advertising—the attention stops. The leads dry up. People stop subscribing, trying, and buying. Traffic comes to a halt.

The good news is that, like your laptop computer or your cell phone, you can charge batteries for your site that store attention and make it available to you even when you're not turning the advertising crank.

Traffic Isn't Cheap

We have many ways to draw people to our websites these days. Our online advertising resources copy the offline world. Banner ads adorn our favorite web destinations, mimicking the ads found in newspapers and magazines. Videos mirror the commercials we see on broadcast TV. Old-fashioned radio ads are delivered digitally to our Pandora streams.

Like pre-Internet days, we purchase space on websites like we once purchased space in print magazines. We pay for *impressions*, or the number of people who *might* see our advertisements. We hope our print ads will be noticed, and that they will drive new visitors to our stores and new callers to our phone centers. Likewise, we hope our display ads will generate clicks and bring fresh traffic to our sites.

Our online and offline advertising has another similarity: when we stop paying for the ads, the traffic stops coming.

Search Ads are Getting More and More Expensive

Search advertising has changed the way we advertise. Search engines know what millions of people are looking for every minute of every hour of every day. They are willing to let us advertise to those who might be looking for a solution like ours, based on the keywords they are entering. But this access comes at a price.

The search engines treat search keywords like raw meat, encouraging businesses to claw at one another like hungry dogs. Businesses bid for the right to advertise to visitors who enter desirable keywords indicating they might be interested in what the businesses offer. Thus, prices have been bid up significantly, especially for highly coveted keywords.

In 2011, businesses in the insurance industry bid-up searches that included the word "insurance" to $55 per click, the most expensive keyword in search advertising. If one in 10 of these clicks converted to a lead—a 10 percent conversion rate—that would mean these companies were willing to pay $550 for each new lead. And a lead is not a paying customer.

In all industries, it's getting more and more expensive to advertise on search engines.

Even "Free" Organic Search is Expensive

If we do a good job of including important keywords in the content on our site, the search engines will get a good sense of what our business is about, and will rank our site well in their main organic listings.

However, there are other factors involved in earning a place on the coveted "page one." Other sites must link to you. You must provide the right types of pages for Google to give you priority. Each page must provide information to the search engines via properly formatted metadata, sitemaps, robots files, and more.

As a result, businesses are hiring teams of experts to ensure that they rank on the search engines for important search terms. Businesses are required to invest in a steady stream of content, as Google has begun favoring sites that change frequently.

Yes, even "free" search traffic comes with a price.

The bottom line is that traffic isn't cheap, even on the web. When someone comes to your site, you must make the most of that visit, or watch the dollars spent on the effort dribble away each time they click away.

What if we could save these visits? What if we could store the interest of visitors who aren't yet ready to buy, try, or subscribe, and tap this resource later when they may be more ready to act? Well, we can. As it turns out, we can build marketing batteries that power our marketing efforts over time.

Store Your Advertising Investment in Marketing Batteries

In a typical rechargeable battery, like that found in your mobile phone, there are three ingredients that work together to store energy and then discharge it. For example, the lead-acid batteries used in our cars combine lead, sulfuric acid, and an electrolyte.

Likewise, your marketing batteries need three components: **contact information**, **permission**, and **content**.

In a marketing battery, content is the key to both charging the battery and discharging it. Here's why.

Use Content to Charge Your Batteries

Marketing batteries store visitor interest *before* visitors are ready to buy. As we said in earlier chapters, we need to give them something to "buy" with their contact information and permission.

Content is one of the most cost-effective interim "products" you can produce.

Use Content to Tap the Stored Marketing Energy

Once we have stored their contact information and permission, we need something to activate them, to get them to return to the site for another chance to buy. Again, we must entice them with content to return.

In both cases, "content" can be informational, educational, entertaining, or promotional. It can come in almost any form.

Isn't this just a fancy way of saying, "You need to collect leads"? If so, why is the analogy important?

Marketing Databases are Misused

Most businesses believe they don't need leads. However, every business knows the pain of spending good money on advertising and seeing nothing in return for it. No, we're not just talking about building a lead database. We're talking about storing and using advertising energy long after the ads have stopped running.

Those businesses that do focus on lead generation don't seem to understand two very important aspects of lead management that are the same for a battery:

1. They only work if you discharge them
2. They dissipate over time—if you don't use the energy you lose it.

Too many businesses fail to continue to communicate with their "leads." Marketing doesn't want to "spam" them with email and junk mail, so they stop the conversation altogether. Then, salespeople cherry pick the leads, contacting only those who are most obviously ripe, leaving the rest to age and wither.

Just as a battery creates an electrical potential, a marketing database creates a sales potential. Unless you *frequently* discharge the potential, you gain nothing.

Marketing Batteries in the Lab

There are a number of ways to build marketing batteries in your business. We will discuss four types in detail:

- Subscriber batteries
- Customer batteries
- Social batteries
- Mobile batteries.

Note that in each case, you must have all three components:

1. Contact information
2. Permission
3. Content.

Subscriber Batteries

The energy stored by an email list is widely applicable, and email is a key strategy in four of the five conversion formulas we have defined.

Thanks to the existence of a large number of email service providers (ESPs), turnkey email batteries can be found at a variety of price points and feature-sets, ready to charge up. Enterprises with very large lists might consider ExactTarget or Silverpop, which offer more advanced marketing automation features. AWeber has a very high delivery rate. MailChimp is integrated into many of the other services I use in my own conversion lab, including Google Analytics.

Contact information

The subscriber battery is charged by a web form, which is usually provided by your ESP. Your content entices visitors to subscribe by completing this form, and their contact information and permission is saved by the ESP.

You can ask your subscribers for just about any information, but that doesn't mean that you should. You can collect a complete contact record: name, phone number, postal address, and other qualifying information. Asking for more information will likely have two effects:

1. It will lower your conversion rate, reducing the number of leads in your battery
2. It will increase the quality of the leads, as only the most interested visitors will complete all of the information.

It is your job to balance these two dynamics, and trying different approaches is the only way to find out how your audience will respond.

Certain kinds of information may reduce your conversion rates substantially, and should be considered only if absolutely necessary. Such information includes the visitor's mobile phone number or their date of birth.

As a rule of thumb, you should only ask for the information you need and will use as part of your sales process.

Permission

Permission can be implied from the act of completing a form (a permission scheme called *single opt-in*), or can be verified by contacting each subscriber by email (a permission scheme called *double opt-in*) before allowing you to email to them.

Single opt-in permission results in a larger mailing list over time, but these lists often have higher opt-out rates and generate more spam reports. People often forget that they granted permission and see subsequent emails as unsolicited.

Double opt-in lists must be verified by the prospect by email. When visitors complete your form, they are sent an email asking them to confirm that they gave permission.

Your double-opt-in list will grow more slowly than a single opt-in list because circumstances conspire to prevent prospects from confirming their subscription. Many subscribers will, for one reason or another, never receive the confirmation email. Others will ignore it.

However, double-opt-in lists are of higher quality, since the subscribers have twice reinforced permission for you to communicate through email. Many ESPs require a double-opt-in to minimize spam reports that may make their customers' email undeliverable.

In general, most businesses will benefit from a higher-quality, smaller double opt-in list, and I recommend this approach.

ESPs will also manage the *opt-out* process, in which subscribers revoke permission, asking not to receive email from you. American CAN-SPAM legislation requires that email recipients be given ways to opt-out of any list.

Content

The subscriber battery is discharged by providing content to the ESP, which sends email on your behalf. This is preferable to sending email yourself, as good ESPs manage relationships with Internet Service Providers (ISPs), keeping you off of spam lists and making sure that most of your emails make it to your subscribers.

Many marketers run "nurturing campaigns" or "drip campaigns" to discharge the energy in their email lists. I hate these passive-sounding terms. These names evoke images of company-focused e-newsletters and image-building content. Yawn.

Would you create different content for an "excitement-generating campaign" or a "prospect-appreciation campaign" or a "trier education campaign?" I think you would.

Which kind of campaign do you want to get in *your* inbox from companies?

A word about choosing an email service provider...

You have many ESPs to choose from. For your digital conversion lab, you will want to choose an ESP that offers:

- *Full analytics* including the open rate, bounce rate, click-through rate, unsubscribe rate, and conversion rate of each email sent.
- An *auto-responder* capability so you can automatically send a series of welcome, how-to, or educational emails to new subscribers.
- An *RSS-to-email* capability that turns your blog into an e-newsletter.
- *List segmentation* so you can divide your lists and send different content to them.
- Integration with your *customer battery* (see below).

ESPs charge for their services in a variety of ways. Some charge based on the number of emails you send. Others charge based on the number of subscribers in your database. Still others charge a flat monthly fee. Consider the size of your list, volume of email, and expected growth when choosing an ESP.

To compare the cost of various ESPs, divide the estimated monthly cost by the number of emails you will send in a month. This will give you a cost-per-email sent for each, and help you compare.

Finally, you will want to select an ESP that is easy to use. If you have trouble sending email due to a difficult interface, you will not be successful in discharging your subscriber battery.

Customer Batteries

Customers generally get treated differently than leads, and this is unfortunate for them and for our businesses.

Contact information

If your business is a brochure, online store, consultative site, or online service, it is common to treat customers differently than subscribers. When a prospect buys, their contact information is usually shuffled off to the Customer Relationship Management (CRM) system. These systems are designed for salespeople and account managers to continue managing the relationship. Perhaps your customer list lives with your credit card processor or in your financial database.

Such systems are not designed for sending email, and are often out of reach of the marketing department. This is a mistake.

It is far easier to sell to an existing customer than to gain a new one. In short, your customer database should be your most valuable marketing asset.

Free this contact information. Give your marketing people access to this valuable asset. Many CRMs will integrate with ESPs or marketing automation systems, enabling marketers to more easily tap the stored power in the list.

Even if your product or service is only purchased occasionally, you have the ability to turn customers into reviewers, raters, and social media evangelists. Authors Robert B. Cialdini, Ph.D., and Dan Ariely have documented an important phenomenon with customers. People tend to feel more positively about what they own solely because they own it. Give your customers ways to express their satisfaction.

Permission

There is an implied permission to contact customers of your business. However, customers should be treated with the respect befitting someone who has helped to grow your business. Always give them a way to opt-out of marketing emails, and ensure that systems are in place to honor all opt-out requests.

You may offer them a menu of contact methods or let them control the types of communication they receive. Some may opt for industry news, while others choose to receive information about your brand.

You know your customers. What would they call respectful and relevant communication?

Content

In a way, you have more latitude with your customers to "be yourself" as a company. Don't limit your communications to new product updates and company news. Consider some of these offerings for your customers:

- Ask them to share with others by providing ratings and reviews. Invite them to join your company on any social networks you participate in.
- Create content or training that helps them use your product better.
- Educate them on complimentary products, even if you will not profit from the purchase of those products. You win when they make the best use of what you offer.
- Share with customers the best content that you create for your prospects and subscribers.
- Ask them to provide feedback to your company.
- Share the most interesting threads from industry forums and invite them to participate.

Be creative, transparent, and authentic with these wonderful people.

Social Batteries

Social networks provide us with a new platform to build batteries that do not have the same level of commitment as subscribers. The social battery is easy to charge. It takes little commitment to "like" a brand on Facebook. As a result, these batteries deliver a lower potential voltage than that found with subscriber and customer lists.

Occasionally, huge bursts of energy will be emitted by social batteries, sometimes with very positive effects. This is the promise of a viral event, an unpredictable upside to social networks.

As of this writing, the most popular social battery is far and away Facebook. In the United States, the top five are rounded out by YouTube, Twitter, LinkedIn, and a surging Google+. A bevy of niche social networks also abound: Pinterest for images, Quora for questions and Plancast for events.

Which social network your business should participate in depends on where your ideal prospects hang out, the kind of content you create, and ultimately, what brings more qualified prospects to your business. All of these questions can be answered in your conversion lab.

Contact Information

Social networks don't share contact information so much as *associations*. Our businesses are not asking for information as much as asking to be associated with individuals. The logic is simple: "Your social media friends must think well of you. If, by *association*, you seem to think well of our business, then your friends will be compelled to think well of us, too."

This lack of direct contact information makes social batteries somewhat finicky. You can't always rely on getting a charge from them. At other times, you'll be surprised at the surge they deliver. As in all marketing batteries, content, shared with social networks, is the catalyst that starts the traffic flowing.

The social battery has one advantage that is fundamentally new in marketing: with the right content, these batteries charge themselves. This occurs when your followers share your content with their friends and connections, who then become friends, fans, and followers of yours.

Permission

In social networks, when an individual likes, follows, or connects with your business, there is an explicit permission granted to associate with them. In general, an individual's friends can see that they have aligned with your business.

Social networks offer individuals control to grant and revoke permission. Facebook allows its members to set their permissions at a fine level, identifying how freely their profile information is allowed to wander. It is also as easy for a member to disconnect from your brand as it is to connect. All they have to do is unlike, unfriend, stop following, or block you. LinkedIn still requires some proof that you know a new connection, and these connections can be severed just as easily as on Facebook.

Ironically, social network participants seem more likely to give up control of their privacy. This seems to be a part of the social culture. If you're not a good social citizen, the network offers a great way for them to disparage you in a very public way to their friends. This acts as a deterrent to bad behavior on the part of businesses that would violate implied social contracts when marketing into social networks.

Content

As I've noted, social batteries are somewhat unreliable energy sources. When you share content on a social network, it joins a steady stream of other's content. These are noisy places.

However, social networks support a rich variety of content. Even the 140-characters-per-post Twitter has add-ons that allow you to tweet pictures and videos.

Take note: Content swims in a stream...

When you post content to a social network, it generally starts on your profile. The posts are then shared in your followers' news feeds or streams. Feeds and streams are a constantly changing flow of content coming from you and the friends of your followers. Your post may not last long, especially if your followers have many prolific friends.

Facebook complicates things further by using an algorithm called Edgerank that places the most "active" content at the top of your followers' news feeds. If your content isn't shared and liked, it may never be seen by anyone. More popular posts will push it down in priority.

In a social network, irrelevant content floats away in the stream, but sharable content has fins. You have to work a little harder on content that is destined for social networks. Here are some tips to consider:

- Write titles for your content that titillate, surprise, or tickle the funny bone
- Favor pictures and images that are visually powerful
- Infuse your content and titles with topical, news-related, or cultural references
- Share and like other's relevant content—these actions follow the same path through social networks that your original content does.

While much of this work results in building relationships and increasing trust, your ultimate goal is to get people back to your website. Each time you do, you get another chance to see if they are ready to subscribe or buy.

Mobile Batteries

Most mobile devices offer access to email and social networks. Mobile phones offer another digital channel that is going to play a huge role in future campaigns: text messaging, or short message service (SMS) messaging.

Contact information

More so than even email, mobile phone owners see their phones as very personal and private. They are reluctant to share their cell number for fear of receiving promotional content via text, or SMS. The carrot that you dangle in front of your site visitors to entice them to enter their mobile number must be highly relevant and valuable.

Permission

Many mobile phone companies charge for each text message sent or received. This means that there can be a real cost to your prospects if you send a marketing message via text message.

You must collect **explicit permission** to send text messages, and be sure to remind the visitor that they may be charged by their mobile service provider before they agree.

Your mobile prospects will require an easy way to opt-out of your communications. Tell them how with each text you send. They should only need to text you back with "STOP" or "OUT."

You will have to select an SMS sending service similar to an ESP. SMS services can be found in a wide variety of configurations. Many are free for small lists. Others charge similarly to ESPs.

Content

Because mobile phone owners still see text messages as a personal, advertising-free channel, your content must conform closely to what you promised when you asked for permission. If a mobile visitor agreed to receive real-time sports scores, you should avoid the temptation to send messages promoting products or services.

SMS messages in general must be time-sensitive and relevant. For example, SMS is a place for online services to deliver notifications about the status of a customer's account. Online stores may be allowed to text shoppers when an out-of-stock item becomes available. These are the kind of real-time, relevant contacts that make the mobile battery work best.

A Word About Mobile Apps

An alternative method for delivering content to a mobile device is through an app. This approach may be particularly good for online services that can extend their site to the phones of those who install an application. Publication sites can use an app to deliver content directly to a phone or tablet. Online stores can use an app to deliver specials and new product announcements.

The mobile app charges the mobile battery by securing permission when the owner installs the app. The battery is discharged by content. The app offers a much richer platform for content than SMS, and even its cousin, MMS (multimedia messaging service).

If you have content compelling enough to get prospects to install your application and use it frequently, then by all means develop an app.

Not All Content Discharges the Same Way

Content fuels your marketing strategy. It charges your batteries, creates a flow of traffic from them, and makes your prospects better buyers for what you offer.

Not all content is created equal. You can't just toss it out there and trust that all is working well. You need to understand which content is drawing people to your web properties, which is creating new prospects, and which is generating sales.

Fortunately, your digital conversion lab is equipped to deliver this information.

Which Page are They Landing On?

Our analytics package is well equipped to tell us where people are entering our site. The metric is called "Landing Pages" or "Entry Pages." For most businesses, the main entry page is the home page. However, when we use content to discharge the energy in our marketing batteries, the pages on which the content lives become the primary landing pages for our visitors.

These visitors aren't coming to your home page. They're not being directed to your "About Us" page. They're being directed to articles, videos, blog posts, and specific product pages. The links you share with your email list, your customer list, and your social networks all bring people to content pages.

A major advantage of this approach is that we can run an analytics report to tell us which pages are most interesting to our prospects, which are shared the most, and ultimately, which generate leads and sales.

Entry Page Topic	Visits	Subscribers	Conversion Rate
Home Page	3,543	202	5.70%
Article on Landing Pages	85	9	10.59%
Subscribe Page	26	6	23.08%
Article on Writing Copy	276	6	2.17%
Article on Simplifying Landing Pages	10	6	60.00%
Article on Personas	311	5	1.61%
Article on Writing Subject Lines	328	5	1.52%
Average for Site			**2.46%**

Figure 7.1: Topics on landing pages really charge the subscriber battery for The Conversion Scientist blog.

Using data from the Conversion Scientist blog, the chart in Figure 7.1 shows how the page on which a visit starts—the Entry Page—influences subscription rates. Clearly, topics covering landing pages (lines 2 and 5) produce a conversion rate much higher than the site average. Articles on writing copy and personas generated many visits, but few conversions.

Leads: Their First Purchase Isn't Your Product or Service

I must admit that I don't really like the term "lead" when talking about prospects for my business. It is sales speak, and seems to dehumanize the very people we are striving to help.

The term I prefer is *customer.*

Why call them customers when they haven't bought anything? Well, on the Internet, no one is going to give you their contact information unless you offer them something in return. They'll fill out a "lead" form if you promise a great report, webinar, or some consulting time on the phone. That's a transaction.

The term "customer" works because we should treat our leads with the same respect that we treat customers who have paid with cash.

On the other hand, not every customer is a good customer. Sometimes we have to fire bad customers. Likewise, not every lead is qualified to buy, and we can politely end the conversation with them.

For the sake of this book, it is important to distinguish between leads, prospects, and customers, so I'll continue to use these terms.

I believe that the first step toward higher conversion rates is to build your lead database and treat these people like customers. So, when you see the word "leads" in this book, imagine that it says "le♥ds."

Converting visitors to leads and sales is the goal. These pages need to work as landing pages. They need to implement the primary strategies that your conversion formula calls for. They must encourage visitors to start the demo, subscribe to the service, or buy related products. In essence, you are advertising on your own site.

Once you see what is working and what is not, you can do more of the things that work, and less of those that don't. It is important that you define "what is working" in terms of your business. If you have content that goes viral, you will see a great deal of traffic. However, viral traffic often will not turn into subscribers, leads, or sales. It is often *low quality.*

You need to know when content is working for your business, not just bringing more eyeballs.

Thus, the analytics reports you create should report which content contributed to conversions.

As you become more familiar with the equipment in your digital conversion lab, you will be able to create these types of reports for yourself.

Charging your subscriber, customer, social, and mobile batteries is generally the work of landing pages on your site. The more effective these pages are, the more readily you can charge your batteries for ongoing marketing power. In Chapter 8, I'll show you how to build landing pages and product pages that turn visitors into customers.

Track the Charge in Your Batteries

Your conversion lab is now set up to track the charge in your batteries (number of people in your list and social networks), and the effect you have when you discharge your stored marketing power with content. You'll enjoy watching your audience grow and reaping the benefits of ongoing sales from them.

Chapter 8
Landing Pages Put Money in Your Pocket

Imagine that you're feeling terrible; I mean really terrible. You go to your doctor who, upon looking you over says, "You must feel terrible." Thanks, doc.

But he has a solution and he writes a prescription telling you, "If you start taking these pills immediately, you will start feeling better in a few days. But don't delay."

You stumble off with the prescription to your pharmacist, who delivers a typical medicine bottle to you 20 minutes later labeled "Notsobadizol 40 mg." Remembering your doctor's advice to waste no time, you race home, pour a glass of water and pop the top off of the bottle.

Inside you see pills of every shape and color. Some are large and white. Some are small and blue, red, orange, or tan. Some are clear while others are not.

What does this mean? Are all of these Notsobadizol? Did the pharmacist make a mistake? And given that time is of the essence, should you take one and hope? Should you take one of each type just to be sure?

This is the same experience your visitors have when you bring them to your home page from an ad, email, or search result. You take them from the specific offer to a page that offers them everything. You require them to figure out your company, its offerings, and the layout of your website before they can find what you promised them in the ad.

Many visitors just won't bother.

The typical home page is a bottle full of different colored opportunities that will inevitably bring the reader to a halt in his quest to solve a problem. When possible, let your visitors avoid your home page.

Alternatives to Home

Every link is a *promise.* Every time someone finds one of your pages on Google, it carries with it a description that sets their expectation. Every time you send an email or post a tweet pointing back to your content, you are making a promise.

"Learn More" is a promise to inform. Even the venerable "Click Here" carries a promise to new revelations as surfers pursue their online goals.

If you believe that keeping promises is an important part of any brand—and it is—then your first conclusion should be, "the pages I bring people to should keep the promise I make."

Home pages are notoriously poor at accomplishing this simple task.

This is the role of the landing page: to keep your promises and move the visitor closer to being a customer, subscriber, or trier.

Would you agree that pages that accomplish these goals belong on your site?

We measure the success of a landing page based on its conversion rate: the ratio of those who take action to the number of visitors to the page.

Why Your Pages Fail to Keep Your Promises

There's a lot of baggage that comes with almost every website. There is the expensive design, the site navigation, and the templates that enforce a consistent layout; the logos, taglines, and other image-building cues; and the sidebars and ads that frame the body of every page.

These components can make every page look like that bottle of multi-colored pills. They obscure the content that keeps your promises and cloud the calls to action that turn visitors into prospects and customers.

The litmus test is simple: Anything that supports the decision-making process belongs on the landing page, and anything that does not is likely to reduce your conversion rate.

Product Pages Should be Treated as Landing Pages

The product pages found in online stores are landing pages, and online stores are clearly tempted to add extra information to these important destinations. Let's try our litmus test. If I am a visitor to a product page for, say, a golf club, are links to golf shoes and golf shirts relevant to my purchase decision? After all, I'm probably a golfer. Yet, we can assume that shirts and shoes are not directly relevant to me, and should not be given a prominent place on the page. Listing alternative clubs, however, may very well be important.

Including standard navigation out of habit—navigation that highlights your selections of shoes, shirts, balls—introduces less-relevant information, distracting visitors from their current path.

Let's consider some other possibilities. Are ratings and reviews relevant to the purchase decision? Clearly the answer is, "Yes." Ratings and reviews have proven to significantly increase conversion rates for many online stores.

However, is a "Write a Review" button appropriate for the product page? I would argue that it is not. It is a distraction from buying, unless visitors are brought to the page with a promise like "Tell others about this product." A separate campaign—perhaps by email—to encourage recent customers to rate and review their purchases would be more effective. Use some of the juice in that customer battery to charge your ratings.

What about listing related or similar products on your product pages? This may or may not be relevant. If the algorithm we use for selecting related or similar products is accurate, such information can help shoppers eliminate alternative solutions quickly, and more confidently choose to buy the product they're currently looking at.

But don't feel obligated to offer shoppers other products to click on. Shoppers who were brought to your product page by the promise of an ad are on a mission. On the other hand, shoppers who find a particular page while browsing your site are exploring. They are well-versed in the use of the back button should they want to find another avenue.

The Product Page Already Has a Big Job to Do

The product page has to work pretty hard, as there are many things the buyer might consider when choosing a product. Shipping costs, return policy, detailed photographs, video, and size or color options all must be presented in the space of a single page.

You can see how important it is to strip away ancillary details, irrelevant navigation, and alternative calls to action (such as social media icons) to make room for the information that is needed to support the purchase.

These same decisions should be considered for the pages that publications use to sell subscriptions, the lead generating pages of consultative sites, and the trial and subscriber pages of online services.

Why Your Pages Fail to Help Your Business

A determined visitor will convert, no matter how hard you make it. Everyone else will generally go somewhere else. How do pages make it hard for someone?

First, the people coming to your site need clear direction. Don't assume they will understand the next step, no matter how simple. Ask the visitor to do something. Calls to action tell readers how to take the next step toward solving their problem.

For an online store, the "Add to Cart" button is the highest-performing call to action. For a publication, information on "Plans and Pricing" will address any questions visitors may have after reading a sample. Those running a consultative site might suggest, "Speak to a Knowledgeable Consultant." And our online service businesses will offer the inevitable "Try it Now."

It may seem self-serving, but you need to start with the call to action when setting out to design a landing page. That said, I'm going to walk you through the process of building the page backward from the call to action to the promise.

Building Landing Pages Backward

Your usual page development generally starts with your site's template. The template is the basic design of your site that every page follows, replete with company branding and standardized site navigation. Before you've started, your page already has marginally relevant distractions built in.

Forget all that. Start with a blank page. Doing so will help you eliminate many of the distractions up front—distractions that keep visitors from converting. Then, follow these seven steps.

Step One: The Call to Action

In Chapter 3, we identified the conversions that move our business forward. They change depending on the formula your site follows.

Your landing pages make those conversions happen. They call visitors to *action*.

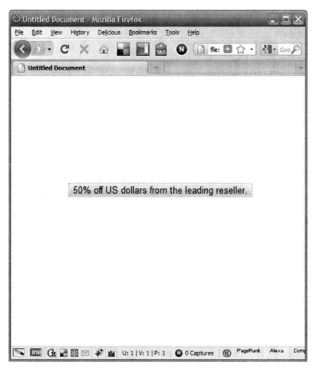

Figure 8.1: This landing page features a call to action.

So, the first step in our landing page design is defining that call to action. Here are some examples for the five conversion formulas.

The Brochure

The "Contact Us" page is the most frequent place we find calls to action on a brochure site. Placing a form on this page offers visitors a way to request contact if they don't want to pick up the phone. Calls to action that work in this setting might include:

"Contact me"

"Request someone contact me"

"Call me"

"Send your contact request"

"Send us an email"

"Request a consultation."

The Publication

The key conversion action for a publication is to become a subscriber. Typical calls to action include:

"Subscribe"

"Join"

"Become a member"

"Try it for free"

"Start your subscription"

"Get instant access."

The Online Store

More tests have been done on the call to action for online stores than for many other of the formulas. Those that perform best in most situations include:

"Add to cart"

"Buy now"

"Add to bag"

"Checkout"

"Add to wish list."

The Consultative Site

The key conversion strategy for consultative sites is to generate leads by providing content. Calls to action are most effective when they are specific, and your consultative site should craft calls to action specific to the content being promised.

"Register now"

"Request the report"

"Download your white paper"

"Subscribe to our e-newsletter"

"Join our LinkedIn group"

"Request a free consultation"

"Get a free quote"

"Like."

The Online Service

We've discussed two key conversions for the online service formula: conversion to trier and conversion to buyer. The most common call to action for converting triers to buyers is "Upgrade." Here are some others:

"Try it now"

"Request a trial"

"Start your 14-day trial"

"Join today"

"Start [doing something useful]"

"Become a member."

Crafting the Call to Action

Regardless of the call to action you choose, refine it to ensure that it is *specific* and *active*.

Calls to action don't have to be short, even if they might ultimately appear on a button. Making your call to action specific is more important. It will be the most visually prominent item on the landing page, so it has to contain as much of the offer as possible. "Subscribe to the Daily Dose Newsletter" should be more successful than "Subscribe."

Adding active words such as "now" and "today" can also increase conversion rates. Avoid generic words such as "Submit" and "Go." And please stay away from exclamation points unless you are working for Yahoo!

Step Two: Fulfill the Promise

Every landing page has to fulfill a promise made by your ad, email link, or social media post. The first thing a visitor needs to see is confirmation that this page is going to do that.

This is the job of the main headline and subhead of a landing page. Like the call to action, specificity is important. However, the promise must answer the visitor's primary question, "What's in it for me?"

The easiest way to start is to copy the text from the ad, email link, or social media post that you used to drive the traffic to this page. For pages that are bringing organic search traffic, grab the text found in the description for the page (the one that will appear in search results).

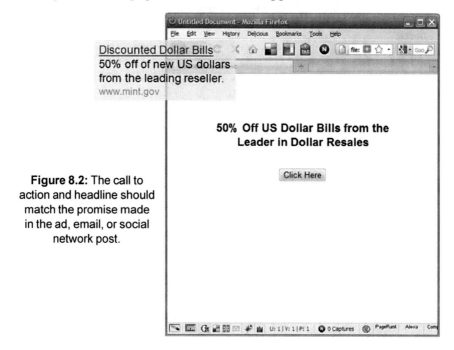

Figure 8.2: The call to action and headline should match the promise made in the ad, email, or social network post.

When possible, include the keywords that visitors may have used in their search to arrive at the page.

Don't let your site navigation dictate the titles of your pages. Remember, every page can be a landing page thanks to the search engines. Just because the navigation link says "Resources" doesn't mean "Resources" should be the only word in the title. Something like "Reports, Webinars, and Podcasts that will Help You Make the Right Decision" is far more specific and enticing.

Always go for the payoff: the *"what's in it for me"* statement.

Step Three: Give Your Visitors Something to Do

As we've said, the call to action should tell the visitor exactly what she will get if she takes action. However, we may want to add a form to the page to gather more information.

The form eliminates the need for the visitor to click to another page, and clearly defines the informational "price" you're asking in return for the promise.

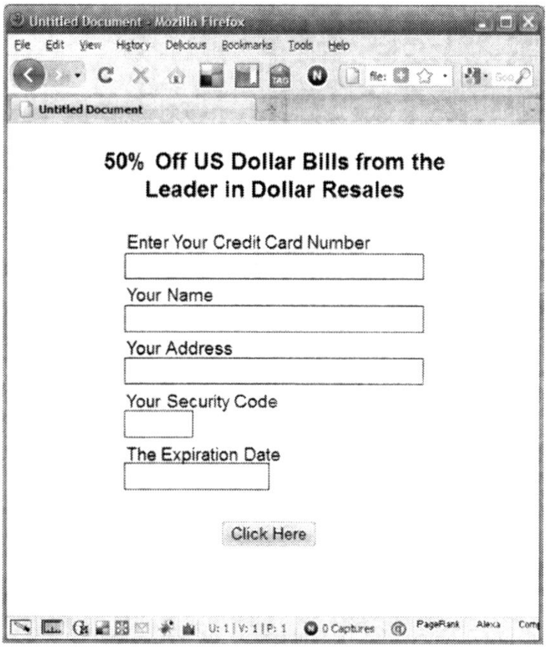

Figure 8.3: Add a form to the landing page to give the visitor something to do.

When designing your forms, there are some things you should consider.

Every Field will Reduce Your Conversion Rate

In almost all situations, the more information you ask for, the more visitors will leave without completing the form.

If you have a consultative site, be selective about the amount of qualifying information you collect. Yes, you want to get the most qualified leads from the site, but only ask for information that will actually be used. Also, take into account the value of your offer. If you're asking for information such as company revenue and number of employees, you better be delivering something really relevant.

Some Fields are Conversion Killers

There are certain fields that almost always give a visitor pause. If you are asking for a Social Security number and bank account information, you're probably not going to have a very high conversion rate.

Other informational requests that cause visitors to pause include:

- Birth date
- Mobile number
- Middle name
- Purchase timeframe
- Income.

Asking where a visitor heard about you is a great idea, but it stops people in their tracks if your list of options doesn't contain the right answer. Instead, use a free-form text area for this, rather than the traditional dropdown menu. The responses you get are more specific, giving you a richer, more qualitative idea of what is driving traffic to your landing pages. And only ask if you're actually going to read their responses.

Long Forms Can Scare People

There are two competing camps in the long form debate. The first argues that you should require as few clicks as possible for a visitor to complete a lead form, subscribe to your content, or purchase your products. Every click is a potential abandon point.

The other point of view is that, if you must collect a great deal of information, you should add more steps—more pages—to your process because putting a lot of form fields on one page intimidates and scares people.

We have studies that prove both of these camps right. Thus, you're going to have to answer this question for your particular audience. Amazon.com addressed this by requiring *no fields* with their one-click checkout strategy.

Start by putting your forms on a diet. Strip out anything that isn't critical to the conversion, or ask for it after the visitor has enrolled or bought. If you still see a high abandonment rate on a form field, consider splitting it into two. We'll talk more about this in Chapter 9.

Stack Your Fields

You will generally get the best results when you organize your forms into a single-column of fields. Even the first name and last name fields should be organized on top of the other. This maintains a single-directional flow down the page for the prospect.

Step Four: Sell the Offer

At this point, you have a call to action and a headline that answers the question "what's in it for me?" But you still have a lot of space to fill on this page. Resist the urge to fill the space by talking about your company and its products.

Really? Didn't a visitor come here to learn more about our company and its products?

Well, no. They came because you promised them something, and you're asking them to take an action that will ultimately help your business. Your goal at this stage is to get them to take action—and nothing more.

You have to sell the thing being offered. If you're running an online service, sell the trial, not the service. You only mention the service to support the person's decision to sign up for the trial.

If you're offering a free webinar, talk about the topic, the presenter, and what the prospect will learn. Discuss your company only if it brings credibility to the webinar.

This may seem like an odd distinction, but it will make all of the difference to your conversion rate.

This is where your copywriter, videographer, and photographer will be critical. They are going to have to work hard to persuade your visitor that the offer is a good one, because you have introduced some serious "friction" into the mix by asking for something.

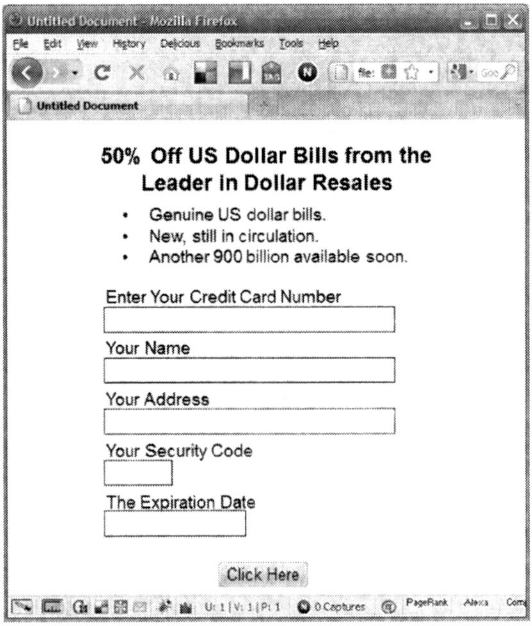

Figure 8.4: Additional copy for the landing page should focus on what is being offered.

Step Five: Overcome Resistance

The moment you ask the visitor to "pay" for something with their contact information or with a credit card, you introduce friction. Friction is anything that gives the visitor pause, confuses him, or makes him resist completing the action.

There are elements you can add to a landing page that will reduce friction and resistance. Most of them center on the question, "Can I trust you?"

This question is especially acute for online stores, publications, or online services that ask for credit card information. Visitors need to feel confident that you are associated with trusted authorities and that others have been happy with your offering. And the more who have been happy, the better.

There are several ways to communicate that you are trusted, and thus trustworthy:

Badges of Honor

There are a number of sources of trusted authority you can add to your page to make visitors feel more comfortable with your business.

- The **Visa, MasterCard, American Express, and Discover emblems** "borrow" trust from these well-known companies. Place these images close to your call to action if a purchase is involved.
- **Policing authorities**, such as the Better Business Bureau, Consumer Reports, and any associations your business is a member of can deliver confidence to your prospects.
- **Verification authorities** will check and monitor your website to ensure that it is safe and secure. These authorities, such as Verisign, McAfee, and eTrust, offer badges for your landing pages, typically for a few hundred dollars per year.
- **Media authorities** who have mentioned your company lend you credibility. These may include TV shows, newspapers, and major websites. It's the equivalent of the "As seen on TV" trust builder used for years in print advertising.
- **Customer logos** provide one of the best opportunities to borrow trust, especially if you have one or more recognizable brands in your client list.
- Not to be overlooked, **your company or brand logo** will carry a certain amount of weight with visitors, especially if you have a recognized brand in your marketplace. I list it last here not because it is unimportant, but to emphasize that it plays only a part in the trust structure of your landing page message.

Statistical Proof

Simple statements such as "Since 1953" tell visitors, "If we weren't good at what we do, people wouldn't have kept us around so long."

Big numbers also can help, and it doesn't necessarily matter what the number counts. For example, you could count up all of the clients you've ever had or all the products you've ever sold and use that number on your landing pages. The meaning is clear: "With more than 500,000 cupcakes served, we must be doing something right."

Social Proof

Dr. Robert Cialdini, in his book *Influence: Science and Practice*, demonstrates persuasively that what we believe about a product or a brand is often influenced *more* by what others think than by our own experience. The opinion of others is a very powerful force in our visitors' decision-making process.

Fortunately, social networks are making it easier to add social proof to our pages. There are several ways to demonstrate what others believe about our offering:

- **Ratings and reviews** are proving to be so powerful a force in the online store formula, that I was reluctant not to include them as one of the key strategies. If you're selling something online, you'll want to give your customers a way to rate and review your offerings. This technique can be used for publications and online services as well.
- **Old-fashioned testimonials** continue to be effective. Using a service like LinkedIn to generate your testimonials is a great way to implement the following best practices:
  1. The testimonial *must* be in the voice of the customer. Visitors can tell fake testimonials a mile away.
  2. The testimonial should include a decent picture of the person recommending the product. Social media avatars are making this very easy, but be sure to get permission.
  3. Highlight the most important part of the testimonial or use it as a headline above the testimonial.

4. Pull your best LinkedIn recommendations and place them on your landing pages. Avoid glowing testimonials and focus on those that contain specifics.

- **Likes, Friends, Connections, and Circles** pose a danger as social proof on a landing page because it gives your visitors reasons to leave the page.

On one hand, showing visitors that many others have "liked" your company and its offerings may increase visitor confidence and make them convert.

On the other hand, it makes them think, "I should go check out Facebook while I think about doing this." You don't want them thinking about anything else but your offer, especially if there are any pictures of cute kittens on their social networks. They are impossible to resist.

Be Secure and Show It

Finally, a Secure Socket Layer (SSL) certificate is particularly important if you're asking for credit card information. This certificate allows you to use "https://" pages instead of "http://" and tells the visitors that their information is being protected between their browser and your website. Most browsers will display a lock or other positive image, which is helpful in removing friction.

Step Six: Show the Product

Roy H. Williams of the Wizard Academy says, "No one buys until they can imagine themselves owning what you sell."

To imagine owning what you sell, visitors must have a mental picture of it. For an online store, this is pretty simple: show pictures of the product. In fact, the more pictures you can provide, and the higher the detail, the more easily a visitor can imagine it in their possession. For other conversion formulas, you will need to apply some creativity, as we've discussed.

Step Seven: Establish a Visual Hierarchy

If you have followed these steps, you have a page with a strong headline, powerful persuasive content, a call to action, a form, trust-building elements, and a picture of the product. That's a lot for one page.

When prospects scan your landing page, they should be able to understand quickly what your page is about and what is important. Landing pages have a very specific hierarchy to follow:

- *Place the headline in a prominent position at the top.* The first thing visitors should see is that they're in the right place and that you are keeping your promise.
- *Clearly indicate that the visitor will be asked to take some action.* The call to action, often a button, must be the most prominent item on the page. Consider using an arrow pointing to the call to action in order to emphasize it. Even if the call to action button is at the very bottom of the page, it should be highly visible.

Don't Send Your Store-bought Traffic to Mark Zuckerberg

I recommend that you remove social media icons from your pages until after a visitor has taken action (i.e., after she has subscribed to your free emails or paid for access to your content).

This may sound counterintuitive to you.

The problem with having social media icons on your homepage, category pages, and landing pages is that they give visitors an easy out. They allow them to avoid the decision to provide contact information or to purchase the product.

Many sites will let visitors take off to Facebook, Twitter, or Google+, where they then become engaged in their friends' vacation videos, political rants, and your competitors' ads. They may never find their way back to the fabulous content you published for them. It costs you something to get traffic to your site. Why send your visitors off to Mark Zuckerberg before they've had a chance to subscribe to your service?

No, the right places for social media icons are on the "Thank You" page, the confirmation page, and in the emails you send after someone has subscribed to your free or paid service.

- *Make it obvious what is being offered.* Accomplish this by placing the "product" images above the fold.
- *Reduce the impact* of trust badges, customer logos, and other graphic elements. While they help reduce friction, these elements compete visually with the headline and call to action. Consider converting these to grayscale images or have your designer screen them back.
- *Make text scannable.* Break up your copy with sub-headlines. Keep your paragraphs short. Use bullets, bolding, and highlighting to emphasize key points of the message. Arrange text into a single column in the center of the page to support the scrolling and scanning behavior of experienced web surfers.

Arranging the Elements of Your Landing Page

Once you have the elements for a powerful landing page in place, it is time to enlist the sensibilities of a designer. The designer need not introduce new elements, and in fact such impulses should be highly discouraged.

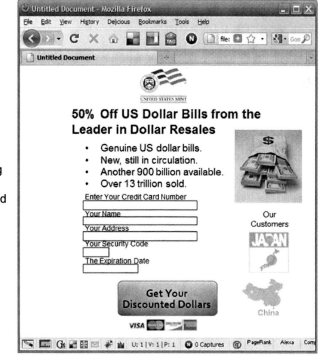

Figure 8.5: The elements of a successful landing page before the designer gets a hold of it.

Instead, the designer should focus on using contrast, position, white space, font-size, and color to emphasize the visual hierarchy that you've created.

The way to create high-performing landing pages is to start with the call to action and support it with reasons to take action. Create persuasive and offer-focused content and incorporate trust-building devices. You'll be impressed with the results.

This all may seem backward to you. In the past, you've always started with the site template and then filled the empty space. The truth is, you have been doing it backward.

Landing Pages in the Digital Conversion Lab

Landing pages are critical to the overall success of your online business. It's important that you monitor these pages' individual conversion rates and try to improve them.

You can make changes to your landing pages and monitor how those changes impact your conversion rates. Any changes you make should be small, as you must be prepared to go back to the previous design if your conversion rates drop.

Landing pages are ideal places to do split testing, a set of techniques that help you find the combination of elements that maximize your conversion rates. For more on testing pages, visit the Customer Creation Equation blog (CustomerCreationEquation.com).

All of this sounds good, but the truth is you're going to run into some stumbling blocks. First, your webmaster or IT department is not usually set up to make frequent changes to your landing pages, or any pages for that matter. Second, it can be messy managing all of the landing pages that you can develop.

There are a number of services available that enable you to create and test landing pages without having to involve your technical staff. Consider adding Unbounce (Unbounce.com) or Lander (LanderApp. com) to your digital conversion lab. These services don't require you to know HTML, CSS, or Javascript, and they provide additional analytics for your lab.

Chapter 9
Keeping Buyers from Checking Out When They Check Out

It's the moment of truth. Your publication, online store, or online service has performed admirably and a visitor has found her way to your checkout process.

The cart is stuffed with items she wants. She has imagined herself owning your content, or she has seen the promise of your cloud-based service. What on Earth could stand in her way now?

Why Ready Buyers Freeze

Imagine that you've followed all the guidance in this book. Your visitor has found a site that anticipates her needs, a site that seems to know her next questions as if by magic. She has enjoyed your thoughtful design, enlightening copy, and clear calls to action. All your promises have been kept.

Then, she clicks "Subscribe," Checkout," or "Get Started." Suddenly she enters a world that seems to have been designed by someone else. The friendly copy and comforting familiarity of the site gives way to very business-like pages.

The domain may be different if you're using a third-party shopping cart. The design may be unfamiliar. In any event, things have changed just at the moment she has committed to make her move.

Now she is being asked questions—personal questions about where she lives, what her credit card says, and if she is a fraudster.

New decisions arise about shipping, taxes, discount codes, and the terms of the sale. It seems as if she must pass a gauntlet for the right to buy from you. It's as if a banker is sitting across from her, studying her financials.

Suddenly, her decision seems a bit rash. Maybe she will wait, just to be sure.

Websites are designed by marketers. Shopping carts are designed by engineers. The transition from shopper to customer has natural psychological boundaries, and our approach to the purchase process seems to exacerbate that.

Many visitors do not survive the transition.

The same thing happens on consultative sites. Visitors are promised a relevant webinar, only to be handed off to a service like GotoMeeting or WebEx, where they encounter a stark registration page on a strange server. The effect can be shocking.

Website managers tend to accept these things without question. Furthermore, the services that provide your shopping carts, registration processes, and subscriptions don't seem to care. What can you do to keep people from checking out when they want to check out?

Is Your Checkout Process Scaring Off Buyers?

To know if your purchase process is a problem, you'll want to examine your *abandonment rate*. The abandonment rate is the number of people who start the process, minus the number who complete it, divided by the number of people who started the process (see Figure 9.1).

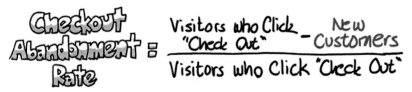

Figure 9.1: Calculating checkout abandonment rate.

If your publication got 10 new subscribers today, but 50 started the process by clicking "Join Now," your abandonment rate is 50 minus 10 divided by 50, or *80 percent.*

Online stores experience another form of abandonment: cart abandonment (see Figure 9.2).

Imagine the chaos if 80 percent of a grocery store's customers abandoned their shopping carts at the checkout stand.

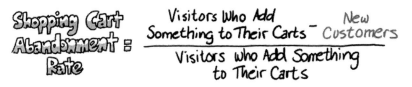

Figure 9.2: Calculating shopping cart abandonment rate.

Eighty percent may seem extreme, but this is not much worse than the average for the Internet, which is generally between 60 to 70 percent.

Your lab is equipped to measure this for you. In fact, properly configured, Google Analytics can tell you your overall abandonment rate as well as which steps of your purchase process are most responsible for chasing away ready buyers.

This is very good news. It means you can examine the pages that seem to cause the biggest problems for your customers and do something about them.

Two Types of Abandonment

Just as science has identified "good cholesterol" and "bad cholesterol," there are "good" and "bad" abandoners among your website's visitors.

Good abandoners leave you as part of their process. They are walking all the way to the edge of buying, even though they are not ready to buy. They are imagining purchasing from you, yet they fully intend to continue comparing your offering to alternatives when they start the checkout process. And they may be hoping you'll hang on to their selections for when they return. Wish lists and persistent shopping carts are a big help to these abandoners. More on that later.

Bad abandoners leave you because they didn't like what they saw after they got started. These abandoners are bad for you because they are lost opportunities. They were going to buy, but you chased them away with your checkout process.

Your purchase process confounded them, introduced new fears, or asked them to do something they weren't ready to do. Many of these abandoners started the process simply because they didn't have all of the information they needed to make their decision.

Forrester Research uncovered evidence of these "good" and "bad" abandoners in its May 2010 report *Understanding Shopping Cart Abandonment*. The report identifies the five primary "drivers" of cart abandonment as:

1. Shipping and handling costs were too high. (Bad abandoners)
2. The shopper wasn't ready to purchase the product. (Good abandoners)
3. The shopper wanted to compare prices on other sites. (Good abandoners)
4. Product price was higher than the shopper was willing to pay. (Bad abandoners)
5. The shopper just wanted to save products in his cart for later consideration. (Good abandoners).

Let's look at what causes bad abandons and then talk about encouraging good abandoners to come back and buy.

Why are Your Abandonment Rates High?

Too often, shopping carts are designed to get the job done—to take a customer's information and complete his transaction in as efficient a manner as possible. Yet, we inadvertently introduce complexity into the process that is unnecessary and unjustified.

Here are the things that are keeping your abandonment rates high, along with ways to fix them.

Caveats, Provisos, and Quid Pro Quos

When we leave the details of a transaction to the shopping cart, we're just asking for abandons—the bad kind. The details of return policies, shipping costs, taxes, setup fees, delivery, availability, and other terms of the purchase lay hidden unless the wary shopper starts the checkout process.

Shoppers know this, and they will often start the checkout process to see if there are any gotchas waiting in the depths for them.

Perhaps the most common omission for an online store is shipping costs. Most of the time, shipping isn't addressed until a later stage of the checkout process. If you're asking for personal information about the visitor before addressing this key question, you are likely to see many of them jumping away or stalling until some outside distraction grabs their attention.

This is why free shipping is such a powerful offer for online stores. Yes, there is a dollar savings for the buyer, but the questions regarding shipping costs have been taken off the table.

Offering free shipping for purchases above a certain amount is another common approach. These types of offers can increase your average order value. It takes shipping out of the equation for those who meet the purchase requirement—but what about those who don't?

Questions about your return policy will also come up. The customer is going to wonder who pays for return shipping. Will she have to get a shipping label from the post office? If her package arrives on day 31, will that invalidate your 30-day return policy?

Perhaps the most effective handling of these issues comes from Zappos, an online apparel retailer who got their start in shoes. They promise on every page of their site:

"365-day return policy, FREE shipping both ways."

That pretty much lets the visitor concentrate on choosing the right product.

While I don't have data on their abandonment rate, Zappos grew to almost $1 billion in sales in 10 years and was purchased by Amazon. com. They aren't known as the price leader on the products they sell, and most of their products are available elsewhere. But, they remove all risk from the purchase, and this has clearly paid off for them.

What can we learn from companies like Zappos?

- Have a free or flat-rate shipping policy, and make it known before shoppers start checking out.
- Eliminate setup fees or introduce them before the checkout process.
- Simplify your return policy. If you have a product that can't be returned, state it up front.
- Raise your prices overall and then be generous on shipping and returns.

- Tell subscribers that you respect their privacy, that you won't sell their contact information, and that you'll give them opportunities to remove themselves from your contact lists.
- Let triers know exactly how to end their trial before their credit card is charged. Offer to remind them ahead of time by email.
- Put the terms and conditions in plain site outside of the purchase process. Use simple language and adhere to the most customer-centric interpretation.

There is a theme in these recommendations: *Don't surprise your buyers when they start the checkout process.*

Abandoners Don't Like Unexpected Choices

Choice is a conversion killer. Like so many things in this book, that may sound counterintuitive. Don't more options give buyers more freedom? The truth is that choice creates friction. It adds doubt, making buyers feel insecure, especially if they don't know the right answer.

Whenever we can make a choice for our buyers, it will generally decrease our abandonment rate. Here are some of the choices that slow down buyers:

You asked them to create an account.

Perhaps you think it's helpful for visitors to be able to create an account on your site. After all, they won't have to re-enter their information in the future, and you can send them specials.

However, most visitors are really just concerned with their current purchase, as well as their privacy. Asking them to create an account asks them to stop and think about something other than owning a product or subscribing to your content. Buyers can choke on the simplest choice.

Here are some ways to prevent the buyer from choking:

- Ask them to login (if they're a repeat customer) or check in as a guest. You can ask them to create an account at the end of the process if they're so inclined to do so.

- Highlight what you think is the best option with a more prominent button, by adding an arrow, or with some other sign that guides them to the fastest choice.
- Make the choice an integral part of the process. Figure 9.3 shows an integrated choice from an apparel retailer with high conversion rates.

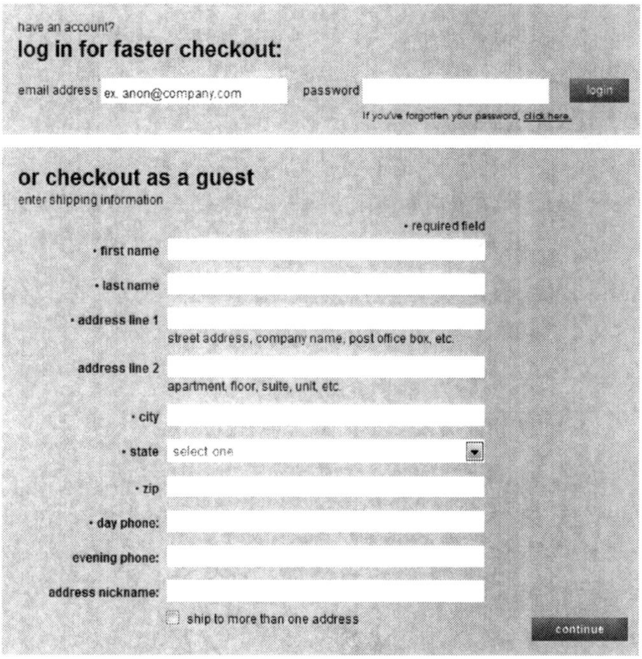

Figure 9.3: This apparel retailer doesn't require a separate decision step and enjoys high conversion rates.

They didn't have a discount code.

Discount codes create a sense of exclusivity for those who have one. However, price-conscious transactional shoppers will get a sense of missing out if they don't have one. Many will go visit one of several discount code aggregator sites looking for a deal, and they rarely come back. The "Discount Code" field is just a reminder to shoppers that they could be missing out.

Add to this the fact that they feel they're paying just a bit too much, and they will abandon the process.

Here are some strategies for reducing discount code abandons:

- Don't offer discount codes. I've seen several sites place a discount code field on their carts "just in case" they want to offer them at some point. Take it off.
- Place the discount code field someplace obscure, like in the lower right part of the page. This requires those with a discount code to search a bit, but they are generally motivated to look.
- Provide a discount code for those who don't have one.

They got freight fright.

Shipping is a fact of life for online stores. Intuitively, we want to give our visitors choices on how and when they can receive their products. However, this choice can stump visitors when they're ready to buy.

Cost is naturally an issue. The folks at SeeWhy (SeeWhy.com) have identified two issues that affect buyers' decision making:

1. The cost of shipping
2. The cost of shipping relative to the cost of the items they're buying.

This relative cost issue makes sense. It's harder to pay $8.50 in shipping for a $10.00 CD. In this case, shipping almost doubles the price. These types of surprises cause the bad kind of abandonment.

To make matters worse, stores add delivery choices. Do you want two-day air? Four-day ground? Seven to 10-day economy shipping? Each comes with different costs, and the decision fatigue can be the death of a purchase.

How can you overcome freight fright?

- *Offer free shipping*—The power of free shipping is not just in the perceived savings, but in the fact that it eliminates one more decision; there's no choice required. The faster you can get the product to the customer for free, the easier the decision is for them to buy.
- *Offer flat-rate shipping*—Eliminate the delivery choices altogether without breaking the bank. Charge one fee for shipping no matter how large the purchase. Your analytics ecommerce data will tell you what your average shipping price is. Consider that as a starting point.

- *Put it in the buyer's terms*—Do the math for them. "Get this item by Monday for $8.95," or "Receive by January 12 for $4.95." This is especially effective near holidays and for products that are given as gifts.

Free and flat-rate shipping may require you to raise your prices. The question to examine is this: Will removing the shipping barrier produce more sales than those lost due to higher prices? Test it.

They didn't think you were going to keep your promises.

You've been to the sites that offer free shipping. It's plastered all over the site. Yet, it is suspiciously absent in the checkout process. "Suspicious" is the operative word.

It's important to keep the terms of the deal front and center once the visitor has begun to buy. Highlight the free shipping throughout the checkout process. Emphasize that any free premium is still included at every step. Keep showing any discounts the visitor received.

They forgot why they were so excited.

Your website is a wonderland of product images, previews, promises, and tantalizing text all presented on purposefully designed interactive pages. Then, when it's time to buy, you replace all of this with forms, caveats, and requests for personal information. It's like Dorothy walking away from the Technicolor Oz and back into the black and white Kansas.

How can you prevent such discontinuity?

- Show the product at every step of the purchase process. Show every product in the cart if the shopper is buying multiple items.
- Repeat the reasons why he wants to buy on the page where you ask for his credit card information.
- Repeat any special offers or discounts at every step.
- Let other shoppers support his decision. This is a great time to pull out testimonials and social proof (see Figure 9.4).

Never let a shopper doubt. Doubt often turns into indecision. Indecision turns into abandonment.

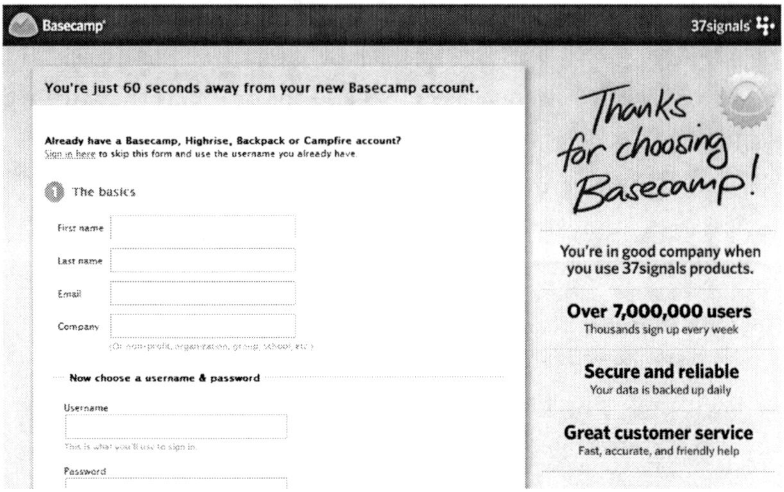

Figure 9.4: Online service 37signals uses social proof, reiterates key benefits, and repeats the offer in their trial registration.

They didn't trust you.

There are certain things that tell us we are "safe" when we're giving personal information to a website. We may not even be aware of how we decided to "trust" a site, but it is a calculation we are making with each completed field and each click.

Here are some things visitors are thinking:

- *Did the domain change when I clicked "Checkout?"* Many sites use third-party solutions for checkout. If the domain changes, any feelings of security the visitor built up may disappear.
- *Is the connection secure?* Many buyers are looking for the https:// prefix in your web address, and browsers are now indicating visually if a site is encrypted for security.
- *Do others support you?* Trust symbols tell the visitor if you're legit. Use emblems from associations you are a member of, logos of companies that have bought from you, and badges from website certification companies. These all lend credibility to your company. Even the little credit card emblems work in your favor.
- *Do you say safety is important?* State your security policy, even if it's as simple as, "We work to protect your information."

Your audience may have unique trust cues. When you know what those trust cues are, you will be able to produce more leads, more customers, and more subscribers. In Chapter 12, *Advanced Curriculum in Visitor Studies*, I'll show you how to identify the things your visitors seek to feel safe.

Resurrecting Buyers After They Leave

You now have some tools to decrease the "bad" kind of abandonment. Is there anything you can do about the "good" abandons? After all, if they're not ready to take action, you really can't do anything about it, right?

Well you shouldn't just wait around for them to come back again. Some visitors just need to abandon once or twice as part of their process. Why don't you help them along?

Save Their Choices

When your visitors return, remind them what they had selected the last time. *Wish lists* and *persistent shopping carts* that save shoppers' choices between visits are two great ways to make a return a pleasant one. Consultative sites can use email to send links to requested informational "purchases," so the prospect can find the content later in his inbox.

Find ways to remember their choices so that when visitors return they can pick up where they left off.

Remind Them They Can Still Buy

Just because abandonment is part of a visitor's decision-making process, doesn't mean she will be good about remembering to come back. You need to remind her.

Start by asking for her email address at the start of your purchase process, registration, or subscription process. Consider placing this request on its own page, and explaining that you'll save her choices for her. You should also disclose the terms under which you will send her an email to secure her permission.

This doesn't have to be as onerous as asking her to create an account. Just get her email address and move her into the process.

If she abandons, you are now empowered to send her an email reminding her that she has a cart full of wonderful products waiting. You can also sweeten the deal. Online stores can offer discounts, online services can offer extended trials, and publications can offer free bonus content.

Ideally, your email will remind her of the items in her cart. However, you can just simply invite her back (see Figure 9.5).

Online stores have reported increased sales of 30 percent from the implementation of remarketing emails.

The process of collecting email addresses up front is going to affect your conversion rates. The effect will be different for every audience. Sometimes adding the request for an email address to your cart will increase abandons. Watch your results to be sure your remarketing strategy isn't significantly increasing abandonment. Better yet, test it.

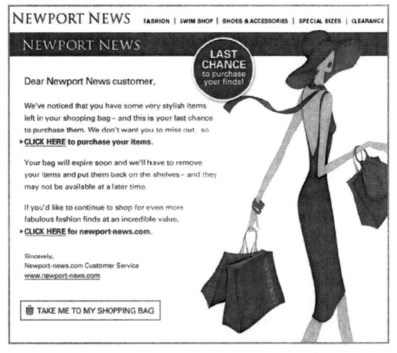

Figure 9.5: Newport News uses email to remind abandoners that they can still buy.

I recommend adding another tool to your digital conversion lab to help you with your remarketing emails. The companies SeeWhy (SeeWhy.com) and Rejoiner (Rejoiner.com) offer tools that watch your buyers and automatically send one or more emails to abandoners. The results could be very good for your conversion rate.

Retarget Them with Ads

Have you ever noticed that you tend to see more online ads for companies whose website you recently visited? If not, start noticing. Many companies are now implementing ad retargeting strategies.

It works like this: When a visitor comes to your site, a special cookie is placed on his browser by an ad network that you hire, such as Google Adwords. These ad networks deliver ads to sites all across the Internet and then advertisers pay them for the opportunity to show their messages.

The ad networks watch for this special retargeting cookie when your visitor comes to one of the other sites they sell advertising for. When they detect it, they will show an ad for your site.

Yes, it's a bit creepy. However, ads for a site someone has already visited can be assumed to be more relevant to them than an ad chosen at random, and retargeted ads generally have higher click-through rates than non-targeted ads.

Like the email remarketing strategy, you can offer ads that sweeten the deal or feature items that were left in your abandoners' carts.

View Your Checkout Process as a Service

It's helpful to see some abandonment as good. It reminds us that we aren't just trying to trick visitors into buying at any cost, but that our purchase processes, registration pages, or subscription forms are part of a service being offered to our visitors.

When you look at your checkout process as a valuable service to your prospects and customers, and anticipate their needs as much as yours, you will find your conversion rates rising and your abandonment rates dropping.

Chapter 10
Getting Visitors Past the Home Page

Conversion rate optimization expert Tim Ash of SiteTuners (SiteTuners.com) defines the job of the home page very clearly: "The job of the home page is to get people off of the home page."

Tim should know. He wrote the book *Landing Page Optimization: The Definitive Guide to Testing and Tuning for Conversions*, and has worked with many companies to improve their website conversion rates.

The success of a home page is based on its ability to get visitors into your site. Like the cover of a magazine, the home page must divulge the information and resources available underneath it, and help visitors find solutions to their particular problems.

While landing pages can respond to specific visitors from known sources, the home page has no such luxury. Your home page must service a wide variety of visitors coming from many different sources.

This is no small feat.

The Battle for the Home Page

The home page, for most companies, serves many masters, and this is why many do a poor job of getting visitors deeper into the site. The home page is a beast of burden and is laden with the goods of many task masters.

First, the home page must deliver a brand image that is consistent with other company communications. Then it has to provide multiple ways to enter the site, from logical tree navigation to specific links to content inside. In addition, it has to show visitors right away how to start their problem-solving process. This makes for a big page, and many will not bother to scroll.

Your home page also may have to serve investors, the press, job seekers, vendors, partners, and other non-prospect visitors.

For many organizations, the home page is political. "We got 250 square pixels more than the consumer group did!" Each manager of a fiefdom within a company expects to keep his precious sliver of the home page for as long as possible. This means that the home page doesn't change much, and that's unfortunate for visitors.

This is a lot of pressure for one page. It's really not surprising that many home pages seem a bit neurotic—schizophrenic even. Too many home pages get saddled with content that won't move the conversion needle (press releases, Twitter comments, fancy animations, and irrelevant stock photography), and fail to offer the most important features to prospects: a strong value proposition, multiple navigation schemes, links to relevant content, and clear calls to action.

Key Concepts in Home Page Design

There are a few principles to keep in mind when developing your home page, regardless of the formula you use.

What is a Home Page Conversion?

First, let's establish what a "conversion" means to an overburdened, abused home page. If we agree with Tim Ash's appraisal, then a home page conversion happens when someone clicks through to another page of the site. Thus, one of the best ways to measure the effectiveness of your home page is by examining the *bounce rate*.

The bounce rate is a measure of the number of visitors who see only one page of your site before they leave you altogether. If your home page is in fact converting visitors into researchers, your bounce rate for home page visits should be low.

Keep in mind that your home page is probably dealing with search visitors who are just in the wrong place and other ne'er-do-wells. You would never expect your bounce rate to be zero. However, if you have a bounce rate higher than 50 percent, your home page is probably not serving your business well.

The Job of the Home Page

If getting people off of the home page is your primary goal, how do you go about this?

You don't really know much about any particular visitor to the home page (remember that it serves many masters); therefore, you must offer choices. Choices can be a bad thing when someone is trying to accomplish something. Choices can create conversion-killing friction.

Thus, the home page must:

- Offer relevant choices
- Help the visitor choose.

Anything that doesn't serve one of these two purposes is either self-serving on the part of the business, or just wasted space.

When you start to imagine all of the scenarios that could bring people to your home page, the *relevant choices/help them choose* model is invaluable.

Familiarity Wins

To quote User Experience (UX) expert Theresa Neill, "Be innovative with your content, but be conventional with your layout."

Her point is supported by a 2011 study by Dr. Brent Coker from the University of Melbourne's Faculty of Business and Economics. The study found that high-converting sites followed conventions, including:

- Company logo in upper left linked to the home page
- Sitewide navigation across the top of the page
- Relevant content
- Relevant images
- Relevant links into site.

Resist impulses to be clever or creative on your home page. Place common elements in expected places.

Honor the "Fold"

There are entire segments of your visitors that aren't going to scroll the page unless they're given a good reason. Naturally, if the reason they should scroll lies below the bottom of their screen—a boundary called "the fold" (named after its newsprint equivalent)—they will miss it altogether. They will probably move on.

Thus, we want to treat those visitors who know what they're looking for with some priority. Who are these visitors who are so resistant to scrolling?

- They are spontaneous new visitors who need an excuse to stick around
- They are returning abandoners who have decided to buy from you and just need to complete the purchase process
- They are people who have seen an advertisement, but didn't click— they only need to find the promise made by the ad
- They are the comparison shoppers who know what product they want, they just need to find the price.

The messages, search boxes, special offers, and links to your cart that these visitors look for should be placed in the top part of the page, above the fold. Furthermore, they may need to be visually significant to capture the eyes of the more impatient visitors.

Those who are researching a problem or trying to get a sense for what your company is all about are more likely to scroll. Put these details below the fold for these more patient and methodical visitors.

Nail Your Value Proposition

New arrivals to your home page need to understand very quickly what your business and the site are all about. This is the job of the value proposition. Despite the fact that the home page serves many visitors, it is reckless to develop a value proposition that has mass appeal. Such generic value statements sound like the posing mission statements that businesses have used to influence their culture.

A tagline is not a value proposition either.

This is the time that you really need your ace copywriter to help you define the one thing **about your site** that appeals to your **best** customers.

This is a key distinction. The value proposition for your website is different from that of your business (unless you are building a brochure site). What experience can visitors expect? Why is this website different from your competitors' websites?

The EcoClean home page (see Figure 10.1) does a good job of combining the company name, an image, and copy to deliver their value proposition: This site will show you what can be cleaned effectively with an environmentally friendly alternative to dry cleaning.

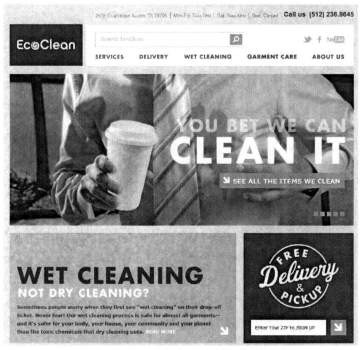

Figure 10.1: EcoClean's home page does a good job of establishing their unique value proposition.

This approach takes bravery. When we get specific about our value to the visitor, we must consciously leave some visitors behind. The EcoClean value proposition will not appeal to lazy yet eco-friendly visitors who just want to clean everything as if they were dropping things off at the evil dry cleaners. Lazy customers' money spends just as well, but EcoClean had to make a decision.

The truth is that EcoClean hedged their bets, and the result probably hurt the performance of their home page. They used a rotating BAH to get more messages onto their home page.

Beware the BAH (Big-ass hero)

It's hard to determine when the BAH emerged as a common component of websites. Early on, these huge images—gobbling up as much as two-thirds of the home page's "above the fold" real estate—extolled the primary value proposition of the website on which they splayed themselves.

As bandwidth improved, the BAH became even bigger, muscling out more and more of the home page's other content. Then came Flash. Now businesses didn't have to do the hard work of selecting just one message for their BAH. They could use Flash to roll one message after another past the visitor. Every few seconds, the hero image would change displaying another enticement to the visitor.

Now, imagine trying to read a book, and someone is waving something in front of you every few seconds. Both your reading speed and comprehension would drop. It turns out that the same is true for home pages.

The motion of a rotating BAH—also called a slider—causes the reader to stop scanning the page and look back up. Almost every test I've seen on this is clear: rotating banners reduce conversion rates.

Nonetheless, this feature is standard on most major websites across the Internet. This is not an excuse to do the same on your site.

Good alternatives include:

- Doing the hard work of picking one message that represents your business and resounds with your most important visitors. Stay focused on what the *website* has to offer, not the business.
- Creating a static, segmented hero shot with multiple messages. For example, a "segmented" hero area might display three product specials all at once.
- Use behavioral targeting to pick the right message for each visitor. For example, when I recently visited one of my favorite office supply sites with all of my cookies enabled, the site knew I was a small business owner and displayed four business-oriented offers. After clearing my cookies, these offers were replaced with more general promotions.

Guidelines like these don't really tell you everything you need to know to build your home page. Fortunately, when you know the conversion formula of your site, you know what should go on the home page.

The Brochure Home Page

The primary job of the brochure site is to make your company look credible to visiting prospects and influencers. Design is important.

You also have more flexibility with the layout, since the brochure doesn't generate leads or sales. If you want to communicate a unique brand image, you can diverge from convention. However, the moment you decide to generate leads with your website, your home page strategy should embrace familiar layouts.

The Publication Home Page

The most important thing a publication site can do is help visitors find the content they want. For a publication site, the home page needs to work like the cover of a magazine (an analog publication typically made of paper).

Magazines use specific stories to get their publications picked up at the checkout stand. Publication websites can likewise select content for the home page based on what visitors will find interesting. Will they want the most recent stories? The most popular offering? The most sensational? Can you present one story from each of these categories?

The home page also needs to act as the table of contents for your publication site. This means supporting a variety of visitor research preferences:

- Logical tree navigation
- Effective site search
- Categorization that makes sense to visitors.

Example: Blog Home Page

Smart companies are implementing blogs as content sources and to woo the search engines into higher rankings.

Blogs usually show the most recent posts on the home page. Many blogs will display the entire text of several posts. Others display teasers of the most recent stories. The latter clearly does a better job of "getting people off of the home page." Furthermore, you can track which post teasers get clicked the most, and make better decisions about what your visitors want.

An example of what doesn't work is the archive of past posts organized by month. While this is commonly found, I question how many people are looking for content by date on a blog site. Consider axing this feature and compiling your posts in more visitor-centric ways: "Basics" or "Most Popular," or "Our Favorite Stories."

Copyblogger provides navigation categories for its blog, including "Copywriting," "Content Marketing," and "SEO Copywriting." Each page contains a summary and a list of posts that expands upon the subject. This is how Copyblogger educates its visitors and builds credibility with them.

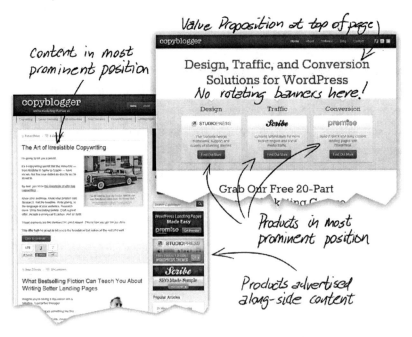

Figure 10.2: Copyblogger.com, before and after. After years as a publication site (left), Copyblogger embraced its inner online store by changing its home page (right).

The Online Store Home Page

If your site sells a catalog of products, your choice of proper categories and navigation are make-or-break strategies (see Figure 10.3). A site that anticipates the variety of angles that visitors to your home page will approach your content wins in the conversion game. A prospect has to find what he is looking for before you can ask him to buy it.

Small Header No Rotation

Functional Categories

Categories Appreciated by Visitors

Content from the Blog

Subscriber List

For frequent Visitors who are more likely to Scroll

Figure 10.3: The Etsy home page must present a huge array of products to visitors. Etsy's home page has helped the company grow, despite this daunting challenge.

If you sell a catalog of products, your choice of navigation and categories will determine how well your home page performs. Like the consultative site, you will have to anticipate the interests of your visitors and put those products in front of them.

The Home Page as Landing Page

There is no law that says a website must contain lots of pages.

Online store sites selling a single product should ask the question, "How many additional pages do I need to support the decision-making process?" The answer may be "one page plus a purchase process."

Do you need a home page that talks about your company and what it does before sending them on to the page that describes your offering? Can your home page be the product page?

If you're selling a small portfolio of products, do you really need a category page between your home page in the product pages, or can your home page function as the category page?

It depends on why the visitors are coming—and visitors come to a home page for many different reasons. A profitable online store will support multiple paths through the site for the different buying processes of the visitors you want to convert into customers.

Whenever we bring prospects to our site, we want to bring them to the category pages and product pages that they are looking for. However, your home page plays the traffic cop for a large percentage of your visitors.

If your site sells a single product, your home page is pretty easy to model. You need a home page that is more like a landing page or product page. For tips on creating such a page, refer to our discussion of landing pages in Chapter 8.

The Consultative Site Home Page

The consultative site home page truly must be a problem-solver's resource. When properly implemented, the consultative site looks a lot like a publication, and should steal from that formula.

The consultative site needs to anticipate the way visitors will learn. An administrative assistant only needs to vet your company on some high-level requirements. A person who is a subject matter expert in your industry will want to know what is new and what will make her better at her job. Existing customers will need training in the use of your solutions.

Your home page should expose a range of tools for these different interests. A logical tree structure is intuitive. A variety of categories for information will be helpful. Search is certainly a requirement for those who don't find what they need, or are impatient.

When in doubt, feature content that does the best job of generating leads. This information is available in your digital conversion lab, and will help you prioritize your home page design.

The Online Service Home Page

The job of the online service is to:

- Get the visitor to try the service
- Get the trier to buy the service
- Get the buyer to login—often.

The online service home page has to manage these tasks for visitors throughout the purchase funnel.

The Home Page as a Trial Landing Page

The online service home page is in fact a landing page for the trial—whether paid or free. As such, it needs to address the visitors' objections to the trial as much as the service itself. That said:

- Place trial offer at the top
- Address objections on the page
- Don't be afraid to address price
- Use proof—social and otherwise.

Place the Login Form in the Upper Right

Make the login very visible to returning triers. Convention says it should be in the upper right of the home page. It should always be above the fold. If I'm coming to login, I'm not going to want to wade through the "try it" content on the page.

Get Them Started as Soon as Possible

Your online service home landing page will make it obvious how to get started right at the top of the page. Offer a few words about your value, and bullet points to define benefits.

Include a call to action button or a short form with which they can get started right there above the fold. The goal is to get visitors to start the process of solving their problem as quickly as possible. Your application should be better at selling them on your benefits than any copy you could devise. This approach will also snare the spontaneous visitors who otherwise would not have spent time with your site or application.

Of course, you need to talk about your benefits for those who need a lot of information before they can take action. Place this information below the fold. Interested visitors who aren't ready to take action will scroll.

Start the Process on the Home Page

If you want to turn a visitor into an instant trier, let him try your application on your home page—or at least let him get started (see Figure 10.4).

Can they choose a user name? Can they answer the first question from your sign-up form? Can they get a sense of how easy-to-use or helpful your application is before they know what is happening?

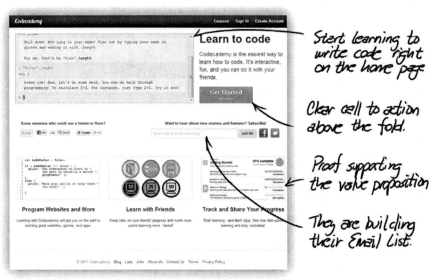

Start learning to write code right on the home page

Clear call to action above the fold.

Proof supporting the value proposition

They are building their Email list.

Figure 10.4: Codeacademy takes a bold approach—it lets visitors begin writing software for the web right on the home page.

Your Designer Probably Led You Astray

Most designers still adhere to Madison Avenue's sensibilities. They probably told you that you needed a site that reflected your brand, that was unique, and that provided a positive emotional context for your visitors.

This is a sentiment that works in print. Brochures are consumed differently than websites. Brochures don't convert well on the web, yet that's likely what your designer designed for you.

If you want your website to serve the problem-solving, information-seeking surfer, it needs to be familiar, conventional, and to work "as expected."

On the web, the best brand experience you can deliver is to provide the information a visitor is seeking in the format they prefer.

There is no better way to build a positive image for your brand or business than to give someone what they want. Period.

Take a look at the "design" of Craigslist.com, a site that is credited with putting several nails in the coffin of newspaper classified ads (see Figure 10.5). It ain't pretty and never has been.

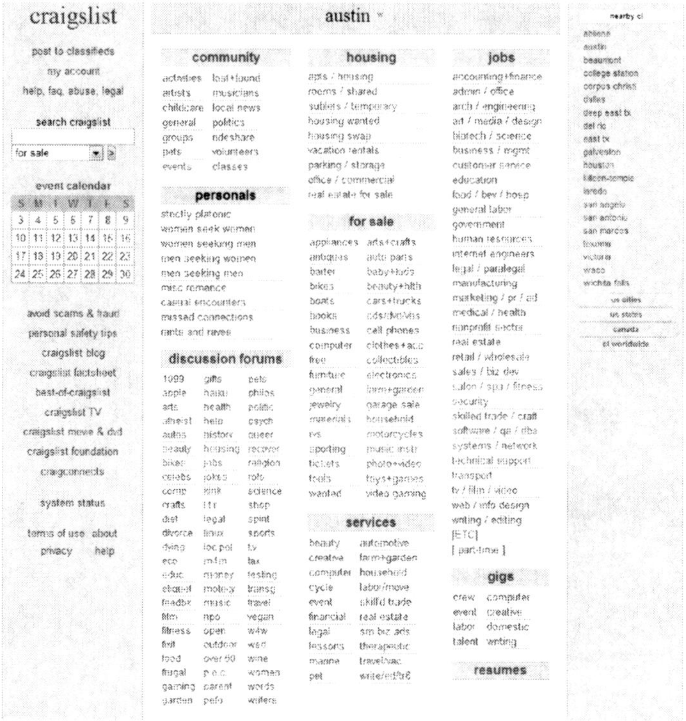

Figure 10.5: Craigslist continues to baffle designers because it breaks so many rules of interface design, yet continues to grow.

Dating site PlentyofFish.com boasts 10 million subscribers looking for love (see Figure 10.6). The site doesn't have a logo or a tagline. No steamy stock photography. No posing slogan such as, "Where lovers come to swim." Yet it has succeeded wildly, knocking industry-leading sites like Match.com off of their pedestals.

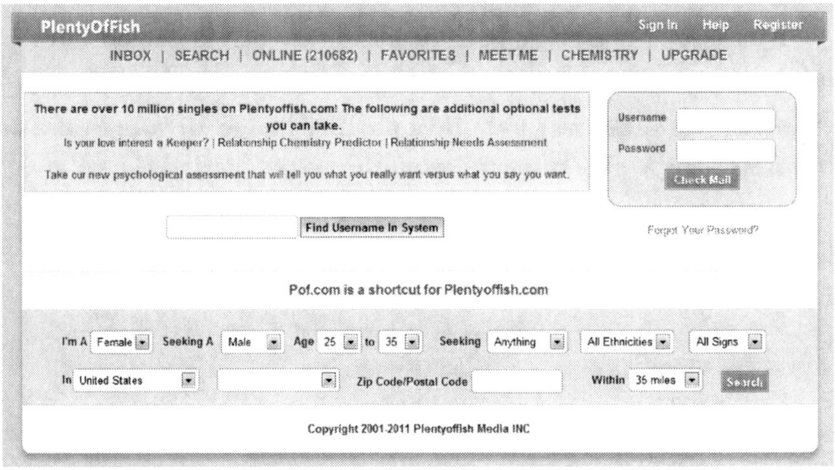

Figure 10.6: Shunning even a logo, the home page of Plenty of Fish seems to work fine for hundreds of thousands of singles.

Mobile Home Pages

Mobile devices are one of the kindest things to happen to web surfers. Why? Because the small screen forces us to create better pages. By "better" I mean simple, single-column pages with clear indicators of what to do next.

However, as smartphones with larger, high-resolution screens gain in popularity, the mobile microsite may be less effective than a full-screen experience. At least one ecommerce site I work with has reported significantly lower sales and conversion rates from mobile visitors after launching a mobile site.

Let your audience decide if you should be investing in a mobile formatted site. If nothing else, it will help you prioritize your home page content. Scarcity of space is a good teacher.

Use Three Key Stats to Monitor Home Page Performance

If your home page is working for you, then leads, subscribers, and sales will increase. Your digital conversion lab, and Google Analytics in particular, can give you a clue as to how your home page is performing.

First, watch that bounce rate. If it goes up, your home page may be under-performing. Also, watch these additional two statistics provided by your analytics service:

1. *Average time on site*—the average amount of time, in minutes and seconds, that visitors are spending on your site.
2. *Average pageviews per visit*—the average number of pages that visitors see each time they visit.

If visitors are spending more time on your site, and viewing more pages during each visit, this indicates that your home page is sending them in the right direction after they arrive.

Chapter 11
Social Media: Finding Music in the Noise

Social media is all about the numbers. The more friends, fans, followers, and connections you have, the more of your content will find its way to qualified prospects. To put it in scientific terms, you are applying Reed's Law to a marketing problem. Reed's Law states that the effectiveness of a network increases exponentially as the number of groups connected to it grows. Each person on a social network is actually a group or mini-network composed of that person and his or her connections.

To put it in non-scientific terms, every person you add gives you significantly larger reach.

The down side to this is that these groups generate a great deal of noise with posts, pictures, links, and other content. Our challenge is to find those people in our network that sing a similar tune. They are our musicians and we are the conductors. The more we can get people playing our tune, the more others will hear it.

Another Attempt to Define Social Media

The definitions of social media change from time to time, from channel to channel, from guru to guru.

Wikipedia—a source I use because it often exposes our collective misunderstandings—defines social media as Internet-based applications "that allow the creation and exchange of user-generated content."

Unsatisfied with Wikipedia's definitions, Brian Solis, social media brainiac and author of the book *Engage!,* came up with the following definition after asking several practitioners:

> *"Social media is the democratization of information, transforming people from content readers into publishers. It is the shift from a broadcast mechanism, one-to-many, to a many-to-many model, rooted in conversations between authors, people, and peers."*

Brian lends this definition brevity with a "short" version stating, "Any tool or service that uses the Internet to facilitate conversations."

In general, the consensus seems to be that social media:

1. Is Internet-based
2. Includes user-generated content
3. Includes interactions (conversations) between people, which may be distinct from "content"
4. Is good for listening to the marketplace
5. Is good for influencing the marketplace.

Brian Solis wrote in a February 23, 2011, blog post:

> *"While conversations are helpful, they are not in of themselves, catalysts to action. It's the conversion of conversations to transactions that leads to organizational relevance and transformation."*

As a Conversion Scientist, I couldn't agree more. I'm primarily interested in the portion of social media interactions that increase conversions, and this must be measurable. My definition of social media conversion is:

> *"Any online interaction in which one person influences the **actions** of another in a measurable way."*

That "person" who "influences" another can be a stranger, or it can be you, the business owner.

The tools people use to interact with each other are social networks. They include Facebook, YouTube, Twitter, LinkedIn, Google+, and many more niche social networks. They also include email, forums, and bulletin board systems (BBSs).

Despite the fact that I've now spent a couple of pages talking about it, I'm less interested in the definition of social media than the strategies that social media platforms and tools offer Conversion Scientists and businesses like yours.

Two Basic Approaches to Social Media

There are two basic approaches to social media: Conversation-orientation and Content-orientation. In your business, one will be dominant while the other will be secondary. My research indicates that using both together delivers the best results.

Conversation-oriented Social Media

This approach is what most social media gurus are talking about when encouraging businesses to develop social channels. With this approach, your employees engage people and build your social channels through conversation.

This strategy is great for customer service, trust building, image marketing, and crowd-sourced support. To be effective, this strategy requires that you dedicate trained employees to listen in on your social channels and respond when appropriate.

Content-oriented Social Media

A content-oriented social media strategy involves sharing content with your social networks in order to get it pushed out further, and to entice people to visit your online properties where the content lives.

Dan Zarrella, author of *Zarrella's Hierarchy of Contagiousness*, says that Twitter tweets containing a link get shared more often than tweets without links. This is important, as sharing is one of the social engines that spreads our message.

A content-oriented social media strategy is best employed by those businesses that have embraced marketing as a publisher. In particular, websites built on publication or consultative site formulas are naturals for this strategy. Yet, any of the formulas can take advantage of content-oriented social media.

To be effective, this strategy requires that a business publish a steady stream of content, and that they have a seed population on social networks to share it with. Ideally, the content is a mix of educational or entertaining content and promotional content.

The content-oriented social media strategy has an advantage in that it can bring friends, fans, and followers back to your website to consume the content. This makes this strategy very measureable by using your digital conversion lab.

To implement the content-oriented strategy, follow these three steps:

1. Create content relevant to your prospects
2. Place it on your site
3. Socialize the content as if it were a product.

Each of these steps has a set of best practices that can increase the effectiveness of your social media efforts.

Content is the Tune Your Social Network Dances To

Your "social graph" is the digital network connecting those that you influence (your business friends, fans, connections, circles), as well as all of the people that *they* influence. It defines your reach, and dictates how far your content will travel across social media.

Content relevant to your industry, area of expertise, and core competency will be relevant to those with similar interests. It reflects the "tune" your company plays. It will be those members of your social networks with similar interests who pick up the beat and share it with others. Essentially, they curate your content for you, from among all the content sources they see.

Thus, content refines a social graph to include more potential prospects for your offerings. It shapes your audience to include more like-minded people, what author Seth Godin calls a *tribe*. You may build a large social graph by sharing witty and humorous content, but without the relevance, that crowd will be less likely to contain qualified prospects—prospects that convert to customers.

Social Media Landing Pages

If you've read this far, you should already be enamored with the promise of landing pages. These are the pages you put in place when you know why someone has come to your site. They let you specifically address their needs.

So, what do you know about your social media visitors? If you're implementing the content-oriented strategy, you know that they are interested in a particular piece of content. Given this very specific information, your social media landing pages must perform several important tasks.

First, your social media landing pages must get visitors to *consume* the content; it must turn them into users of your site.

Next, you want visitors to form an *opinion* of your content and—by association—your company.

Finally, you want visitors to *share* your content. Sharing is important because it's likely that a percentage of each visitor's group is qualified to be prospects—prospects who may be looking for solutions to the types of problems your company solves. You are more likely to get the attention of these prospects if your content reaches them through sharing.

Consumer, opinion holder, and sharer—these are the phases through which your social media landing pages must take your visitors.

Creating Consumable Content

While it is clear that relevant content gets read, we also must acknowledge some truths about social traffic that will influence how we present our content.

First, most of this traffic is coming because they are interested in your content. However, they're not necessarily on a mission to solve a problem related to your business. This same content will draw search engine traffic, which is more typically made up of searchers in a problem-solving mode, but we can't make the same assumption about those who are coming from our social networks.

For example, major brands are finding it very difficult to engage Facebook visitors who have become fans of their brand. Many have closed their Facebook stores for lack of attention. Keep reading and you will not suffer this fate.

Social media landing pages are most effective when they present content in a scannable or visual manner. This explains why articles and posts that start with a number do so well with social media. Titles that begin with "6 Ways," "12 Things," or "10 Reasons" promise a scannable list of tips.

It also explains why infographs and infodoodles are so frequently shared; they offer information in a visual way that is easy to consume.

Such content may be unsatisfactory for someone researching a problem. That's okay. At this point, your main goal is to get your content read, considered, and shared.

Influencing Opinion

There are two primary ways our opinions are swayed: by *our own experiences* and the *opinions of others.*

As I have pointed out, our own experiences are often trumped by the opinions of others, and this is one of the important realizations that our social media landing pages must consider.

If you've done your homework and have presented relevant content in a way that is easy to consume, you will be giving your social visitors a positive experience to talk about. However, you can also let them know what others are saying about the content. This is the job of comments, Like buttons, Plus One badges, Digg counters, and myriad other cues that show social support of an article or post (see Figure 11.1).

Figure 11.1: Social proof in the form of widgets and badges.

These badges can give weight and credibility to your content and, with the right call to action, can make it easier for influencers to decide to share.

Generating Talk

After your visitor has read the content and formed an opinion, your social media landing pages must provide ways for sharing to happen. The classic example of this is the comment feature on a blog page. Readers expand and spread your content by adding to it, and the comments influence what other readers think of you.

Thus, a simple blog page creates a joyous ecosystem of sharing and opinion-making.

There are additional ways to share that spread the content beyond readers and commenters. The same badges that extoll the number of likes, fans, and favorites you have also enable readers to do the same with a click.

Wait a minute. In Chapter 8, I suggested that these be eliminated from your landing pages. Why am I changing my story now? Because sharing is relevant to the social visitor—and we know that a social animal is visiting the page. This is not necessarily true of those who click on an ad. Thus, it will benefit you to give your social visitors tools to talk about your company and spread your content—tools you wouldn't put on a landing page for an ad.

Influencers Earn Their Reputation

A percentage of your visitors will qualify as "influencers." These visitors are not only looking to find good content, they are looking for ways to *make it their own*. They see their actions as a reflection of who they are as people, a way to define themselves by associations with online content.

Thus, it is important that you ask your influencers to act. It is smart to place questions or calls to action within your content, asking influencers to weigh in. A simple prompt is all it takes:

"Have you experienced something similar? Let us know in the comments."

"Tell us how you have successfully used these techniques."

"In what other ways can these principles be applied?"

If you are an influencer, you may have felt an urge to respond to the above calls to action. If so, you are of great value to the conversion cause!

Pinterest is a site that is all about influencers. Pinterest aficionados plaster images all over their pages as if wearing them themselves. With just a scan, you can gain interesting insights into who a person is by his or her pinboards. Influencers love this.

Because of their built-in generosity, influencers often have larger social networks, so their sharing can be very valuable in getting more readers to see your content. Pitch to your influencers and your content will soar across space and time.

On-network vs. Off-network Landing Pages

While I love blogs as social media landing pages, they have one major disadvantage: they require visitors to leave the familiar safety of their social network. This is a disconnect for visitors. Gone is the familiar design and the presence of friends. In its place is a foreign site of questionable trustworthiness.

This is a disadvantage of *off-network* destinations. Studies have shown that conversion rates are higher when Facebook ads take clickers to a destination on Facebook. For this purpose, you should consider building *on-network* social landing pages. You will probably experience the same phenomenon. You can expect your content to be more freely shared and commented on if you keep the visitor within Facebook, LinkedIn, or Google+.

Furthermore, all of the familiar sharing tools—liking, connecting, messaging—are built into these on-network pages, so you don't have to add them to your site.

The disadvantage of on-network landing pages is that they are full of distractions, including ads that may be from your competitors.

Your choice of an off- or on-network destination for your content is largely dependent on the social network itself. Facebook offers a fantastic facility for developing landing pages. Facebook pages allow you to put almost anything you want within them, and to measure their success through your conversion lab. If you are building a social network within Facebook, there is good reason to create on-network landing pages.

However, you have fewer options on other social networks. On LinkedIn, for example, you must create a group. This group is not easily customizable, and there are few opportunities to *invite visitors to become customers*, a feature of social landing pages that we'll discuss next. Likewise, Twitter, Google+, YouTube, Quora, and others offer few opportunities to customize pages to the extent that Facebook allows.

Perhaps the only "social network" that gives you more control of on-network landing pages is email. In this case, on-network means in the reader's inbox, and your email is the page.

To summarize, the choice of on-network vs. off-network landing pages depends on how much control a particular social network offers. And, as we shall see, it also depends on the "turn," or that point at which we ask our social visitors to become subscribers or customers.

The Turn: Switching from Pull to Push

Social media is inherently a "pull" medium as opposed to a "push" medium. We seek to pull qualified traffic into our sphere of influence using content, games, contests, and other incentives.

This technique sits in contrast to interruptive advertising, in which a banner ad, TV commercial, print ad, or billboard tries to *push* a message into our awareness.

Because social media is a noisy space, we find that push advertising works poorly, but pull advertising works quite well. That is why I am such a fan of content-oriented social media marketing.

However, we must at some point execute a *turn*, from pull to push. At some point we must ask for something from our audience. If we don't ask, we don't convert.

Your content may be free, but you create this content in the service of your business. Likes and shares are of little value if you aren't converting social traffic to leads and sales. It is important that your content be peppered with offers to convert. This can come in a variety of forms.

Advertise on your own blog.

Offer ads in the sidebar of your blog that encourage visitors to buy from you or to sign up for special content by email.

Place calls to action in your content.

Put links to product pages, landing pages, and more in your copy, in your videos, and in your social media posts. For example, a call to action placed at the end of an article will be seen by someone who's read the entire thing, and this is an indication that the content was very relevant. They may be well-qualified.

Ask visitors to pay for prime content with contact information.

Don't give all of your content away for free. Require registration for your premium offerings to build your database of qualified leads. This can be done right on Facebook pages.

Use Facebook applications to collect contact information.

When we began marketing this book, we created a Facebook application to start building our own list of interested potential readers—a "reader battery" of sorts. We offered a free video that outlined the five conversion formulas discussed in Chapter 3 (see Figure 11.2).

To watch the video, Facebook visitors had to allow a simple video application to be installed. In doing so, they were asked to give us permission to collect their name and email address from Facebook, and to send them email. There was no form to complete.

This is proving to be an effective social media landing page, and a great way to get invited into the inboxes of interested potential readers.

Place calls to action on your profile.

It is traditional to use your Twitter, Facebook, or Google+ profile to tell visitors who you are and to link to your primary website. But why not offer visitors something and link to a landing page instead? This lets you offer something more targeted, more helpful, and potentially more relevant.

Twitter allows us one link in our profile. Consider using the link to take the visitor to a landing page offering something that might appeal

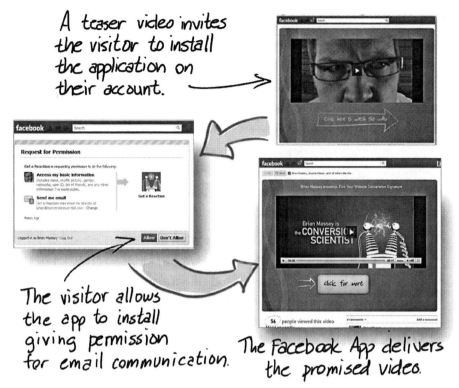

A teaser video invites the visitor to install the application on their account.

The visitor allows the app to install giving permission for email communication.

The Facebook App delivers the promised video.

Figure 11.2: Facebook applications provide contact info and permission without the visitor having to complete a form.

to Twits. In Facebook, create a default page that makes an offer of free content. In Google+, embed links to your best articles within your description.

Turn your profile pages into social landing pages that work to generate leads and sales from your social graph.

Create special interest groups.

One of the key functions of social networks is to create groups of like-interested people. Most social networks offer the ability to create these groups and to invite people to join. On LinkedIn, creating groups is a great way to share relevant content and provide links to your landing pages. Google+ offers circles. Twitter provides lists. Pinterest offers shared pinboards.

These groups offer new places for you to place your content and invite social visitors to come to your site where you can begin a more intimate conversation.

All of these social strategies can work. You should pick those that seem the most natural to your business. Some may require more resources than you have. Others may seem intrusive to you.

Keep in mind that a percentage of your social audience needs your solution and is seriously interested in what your company offers. Don't let them down. Present ways for them to take more decisive steps toward becoming a prospect and a customer.

Using Social Media to Charge Your Subscriber Battery

In Chapter 7, *Charge Your Marketing Batteries for More Sales*, I told you about building social batteries and subscriber batteries that save up marketing and advertising potential for use over time. If you haven't figured it out, I have a preference for the subscriber battery. It is harder to charge, but delivers a more reliable current to your bottom line than social batteries.

The Case for Email

So, why do I prefer email over social media? First of all, I'm not saying, "Email *instead* of social media." What I am suggesting is that email offers a more personal and immediate way to build a relationship with prospects and customers.

The primary reasons why email is critical are:

- Tweets and posts have short lifespans
- Email subscribers are more committed because they must provide personal information and confirm their engagement (double opt-in)
- Your email list is an asset you own and control.

Social media posts have a short lifespan.

The lifespan of a social media post is very short. A 2010 study by Sysomos, Inc., found that the lifespan of a tweet was an hour or less, with 92 percent of retweets happening within that time. However, the study found that only six percent of tweets were re-tweeted. Those that don't get re-tweeted quickly get lost in the noise after a few minutes.

The good news is that, according to Dan Zarrella, tweets containing links are more likely to be re-tweeted. So if you're sharing links to the content on your site, your social media posts should live longer and drive more traffic.

Research by popular link-shortening service Bit.ly puts the "half-life" of a post on Facebook or Twitter at three hours if it contains a link.

Email, on the other hand, lives until its recipient deals with it. This is why email spam is so intolerable. An email inbox is a much more personal space and we as marketers must respect that. If we are welcomed into our prospects' inboxes and provide relevant emails to them, our messages will get read and visits to our site will increase.

Email subscribers are more committed.

The decision to like, follow, or plus-one you is much easier than the decision to provide you with an email address. Thus, we can assume that somebody who has subscribed to you via email is more interested in hearing from you.

This is a key distinction. In social media, quantity counts. In email, quality counts. The effectiveness of the social network increases as the number of members increases. The bigger the network, the more likely it is that somebody will read and share what you are posting.

With email, relevance is important. If you have an "unshaped" list, with people who don't really care about your content or your products, you run the risk of being reported as spammers. This decreases your ability to email to anyone.

With email, we want to shape our lists so they contain only those who have expressed interest in our products, or who have bought previously.

The results are clear. Click-through rates and conversion rates for emails are higher than those for social media posts in almost every industry.

An email list is an asset you own.

Access is an asset. Your email list is an asset, just as a piece of equipment or inventory is. Other businesses will pay you for access to your email list. If you sell your business, you will receive something for your email list. And your email list cannot be taken away from you.

This cannot be said for a social network. Those businesses that have gotten too aggressive with their social media networks have had them shut down with no explanation. Social networks are free to change the terms of their services and to remove features, both of which can limit access to your audience.

You want to build on your own "property," not on the property of someone else.

Click-through rates and conversion rates are significantly higher for email than for social media in almost every case I've seen or researched. Social media cannot deliver the highly targeted one-to-one communications that are required by publications, consultative sites, and online services. And, email continues to be one of the most highly rated marketing investments for B2B and B2C marketers year after year.

Exporting Social Connections from Social Networks

When someone friends you on Facebook or connects with you on LinkedIn, they extend an implied permission to interact with them. Those who set their permissions to allow you to access their email addresses are extending this implied permission to email contacts.

LinkedIn makes it very easy to export the name, email address, company, and title of any of your connections that have their permissions set appropriately. You can import this list into your email service provider (ESP), adding these contacts to your subscriber battery. As of this writing, you can extract Facebook contacts and their email addresses directly into a Yahoo! Mail account.

The implied permission is thin at best. Subscriber batteries with low permission levels don't deliver much of a charge, and you may find yourself with high opt-out rates and spam reports.

I recommend that you not simply dump these social contacts into your list, but only add those that come with explicit permission to send them email. Here's how you do that.

Using your ESP, put these exported contacts into a separate list. Then, send them a special email asking them to subscribe to your list. Remind them that they had friended you at some point, and offer a link to a landing page that lets them subscribe explicitly. Since content is the way we charge batteries, include a relevant article with this invitation email. Choose something that your conversion lab shows has gotten a lot of attention in the past.

Send this email twice. Then delete the list. Those who subscribe have been added to your main list, and have given you explicit permission to contact them by email. More importantly, they have identified themselves as potentially qualified prospects.

Charge Your Subscription List with Facebook Applications

Facebook applications are not difficult to create with the help of a knowledgeable developer. There are a number of services that make it very easy to create these apps with no technical help. They allow your business to deliver premium content, games, and entertainment directly inside the Facebook platform.

Each person who clicks on a link to your application must grant the app permission to access and use his or her profile information. However, when they do, they will have provided both contact information and permission in one step. At this point, your application will deliver their contact information to your ESP, through which you can contact them in the future.

Any Facebook member can revoke permission by uninstalling the application, but the information in the subscriber database is unaffected until the member opts-out of your list.

If you create an application on Facebook, you gain access to the contact information of each person that installs your application. The list of things you can retrieve is impressive, and a little bit scary. Depending on the privacy settings of each individual, this information includes name, email address, birthdate, home town, schools attended, employers, photos, posts, and more.

You also can ask for the right to post things to the member's wall, an action that is visible in all of their friends' news feeds. This can be a powerful tool for spreading content, but it requires a more advanced application.

Control and Track Your Social Media Strategy

Odds are good that your social battery will live on more than one social network. Facebook, YouTube, LinkedIn, and Twitter are just the largest. If you have a technical audience, you may find them on Digg or Reddit. If images or photography are your business, Flickr or Pinterest may be part of the equation.

Each social network has its own analytics reports. Facebook and YouTube have their *Insights* pages with graphs of visits, views, likes, wall posts, and more. You'll find something like this on almost every social network and video site you might use.

Our conversion lab is equipped to track content through all of the visits and conversions it generates. Homing beacons are a great tool for tracking content shared socially.

However, with multiple social networks, multiple sources of analytics, and a weekly stream of content, things can get a bit hairy. For this reason, there are some additional tools you'll want in your digital conversion lab.

There are services that will help you schedule, launch, and measure your content across a wide variety of social networks. HootSuite (Hootsuite.com) is a low-cost tool that gives you the ability to send content to multiple social networks. The paid version integrates with Google Analytics. Online service Spredfast (Spredfast.com) plugs into a wide variety of social networks and even allows the addition of homing beacons to your links for Google Analytics tracking.

These types of tools are critical to an effective content-oriented social media strategy. Your team is going to need them to maintain the momentum that this set of strategies requires.

In general, you should automate whenever you can.

Chapter 12
Advanced Curriculum in Visitor Studies

In laying the groundwork for high conversion rates, massive lead generation, or amazing online sales, you must do three things:

1. Stop spending money on strategies that don't work
2. Spend more money on things that do work
3. Stop boring your visitors and making them feel stupid.

While few will be surprised by this list, it does highlight a very important benefit of conversion-oriented websites: they are often cheaper to build and run.

Your challenge is to find out what works, what doesn't, and what will interest and excite your visitors.

If you try to please everyone who might come to your site, it will be very difficult to decide what and where to spend your money. You would also have to communicate at a very high level. This results in a kind of watered-down website that satisfies no one.

The exercise outlined in this chapter will help you give your site focus and make tough decisions. It is a powerful process, and the beginning of a shift in thinking that will pay huge dividends for your online business.

The first step is to admit that your opinion doesn't matter.

You Don't Get a Vote

Everyone hates popups—at least that's what everyone says. However, something else is going on here. Popups reliably increase conversion rates, especially for charging your subscriber battery.

Popups work like this: you arrive at a website and before you can do anything, a window opens over the site asking you to buy something or subscribe to a newsletter.

If popups were universally rejected by visitors, we would see a sharp increase in the bounce rate when we added popups to our pages. We also would see a decrease in subscribers, trials, leads, and online sales.

Figure 12.1: The popup box on Dan Zarrella's blog would certainly be rejected by his social media audience. But it wasn't.

We typically see neither.

In experiment after experiment, popups increase subscription rates without significantly increasing bounce rates. How can this be if everyone says they hate popups?

This is just one example of how our preconceived notions can mislead us. Popups turn out to be a convenient way for visitors to start a conversation with us, and those who aren't ready to do so have no problem simply closing the popup to reach the content they want.

There will be some visitors who turn away when they see the popup. That's okay. This usually indicates they aren't committed anyway.

People who subscribe are more likely to return and more likely to buy your products. **You must be willing to lose the visitors who won't subscribe, to make it easier for those who will.**

In other words, you're going to have to walk away from the tire-kickers and hangers-on to better serve those visitors who make up your core audience.

This might seem hard to do, but this chapter will show you how. This chapter, more than any other in this book, will help you increase your fortunes online. Pay attention.

Forget What You Know About Your Customers

Every marketing book, every online sales blog, and every guru will tell you that you have to know your customer to market to them effectively.

I don't disagree, but I'm going to tell you something different: What you *think* you know about your customers is actually hurting your business on the web.

More than any other marketing channel, visitors to the web are coming for a reason. Your job is to understand those reasons, and only focus on those you can help profitably. You must let the rest go or risk being irrelevant to everyone.

Here are a few guidelines that may help you let go of some of your visitors:

- If they don't own a computer or a smartphone, ignore them.
- If they don't have the problem that your product or service fixes, then let them back-button out of there.
- If they don't use the Internet to make decisions about solving the problems you solve, let them go.
- If they won't be comfortable with your company culture or values, set them free.
- If they are unprofitable for the business, fuggedaboutit.
- If they take a long time to close, or are reluctant to buy online, drop them like gravity.
- If most of them are women, don't worry about the men. And vice versa.
- If they found your site by accident, or are just browsing, let them waste someone else's server time.

Who does this leave?

It leaves a man or a woman who is somewhat comfortable with the web, has access to it, uses it to make decisions, has a problem for which you have a solution, is comfortable dealing with people like you and your employees, and is willing to pay for a solution to their problem.

I'd say that any site that appeals to this visitor is going to have some serious success.

The visitor your site is currently selling to probably looks more like this:

They are both a man and a woman. They live everywhere you can reach. They are free with their money and also very price-sensitive. They are coming because they want to learn about your company. You don't care how they found you, as long as they are here. They are buying for themselves as well as for a business. They like everything you like and hate everything you hate. They don't understand that they need your product, so you must explain it to them. They like to spend their time reading about companies like yours.

This person does not exist, yet you probably spend much of your web real estate selling to him. You may believe you are selling to a broad audience, but you can't.

If you try to sell to everyone, you sell to no one. It's time to pick your target customers.

Targeting your best customers means stepping away from the others. Most of us aren't comfortable with this. Fear not, for I have some guidance for you. To paraphrase author and ad man Roy H. Williams, your website has three or four visitors coming from thousands of different computers.

This chapter is about identifying and then connecting with the visitors who will grow your business. This knowledge cannot rest with a few, but needs to be in the hands of your marketers, writers, designers, information architects, and search engine optimizers. When the entire team is creating for the same people, your site becomes consistent in voice and design. It becomes specific in addressing key visitor concerns.

And it converts like gangbusters.

Here are the steps to develop your portfolio of *visitor personas*. These personas will guide your team to higher conversion rates and more sales.

Target Your Best Visitors

Ultimately, you will want a portfolio of personas to guide almost all of your decisions about your website. Now ask yourself, "Which customers are going to make our online business rock?"

Which visitor would be easy to close?

Which visitor buys the most expensive items?

Which visitor has the longest lifetime value?

Which visitor is most likely to talk to others about our company?

Which visitor is already a customer?

It's helpful to choose personas that represent each of the four modes of research that we'll discuss below, if relevant. Doing so will help you round out your content.

Identify Triggers

To help you narrow down the first of your prime visitors, you need to understand what happened in their life that made them type in your web address or enter a search that revealed your website.

"It could be lots of things," you say. I know. But, imagine the scenarios that would result in them being *most likely to take action* on your site.

If you sell shoes, you may say, "They got a date with Mr. Right and have four days to buy the perfect shoes for that dress."

If you sell IT services to enterprises, you might say, "The IT manager was just asked to cut 20 percent from his budget or the CIO will do it for him."

If you are an online university, you may say, "A young man just found out his wife was pregnant, and his minimum-wage job isn't going to be enough to raise a family."

Yes, these all sound painfully specific. You are certainly asking, "What if someone comes for a different reason?" Many will.

These triggers will get generalized as your team implements your website. This is inevitable. But if you start without a specific target in mind, you can expect your web content to become generalized—so much so that it becomes light, airy, and ineffective, like a cloud dissipating on a hot summer day. It's better to start with very specific targets.

Specifics build empathy. Empathy leads to communication that generates action. Action means conversion. When in doubt get *specific*.

How to Lie (and Tell the Truth) Effectively

The best liars and con artists will tell you that the way to dupe someone is to regale them with details, even made-up details. Specifics help the listener fully imagine a scene that never happened. When someone has imagined a situation completely, they may as well have been there themselves. This is the advantage of the con artist.

It also plays into the hands of effective marketers who are telling the truth.

Be elaborate when you want to be persuasive. Details that don't seem important should be included if they help complete an image in the reader's mind. Don't state that you have a world-class data center. Tell us how many servers are in the data center? What does it take to cool the place? Who is the manager and why is he the guy who is qualified to protect our digital data? What are his quirks?

Once we can picture a very human and very determined person watching over a world-class data center, we can more easily imagine our data—and our dollars—going to his company.

Compose a Customer Commentary

Once you've identified the triggers, it's time to craft your customer commentaries. A customer commentary is the visitor's story written in his or her own words.

The customer commentary is a tool so powerful that it causes almost instant enlightenment when read. That makes it an indispensable tool when you're trying to get everyone on your team on the same page. It's your chance to fully realize your hallmark visitors and completely understand their thinking.

Imagine one of your best customers. Write out what they would say if you interviewed them, in as much detail as you can. Now notice how some of the things you're doing online just won't work for them. This is an important result.

Let's take the example of our young man whose wife is pregnant and who is visiting the site of an online university.

- Was he surprised by the pregnancy or were they trying?
- Does his wife work? Will she work after the baby comes?
- How does he feel as a man?
- What topics interest him?
- Was he a good student in high school?
- Are they newlyweds or have they been married a while?
- What kind of support do they have from their families?
- What trust issues does he have with online universities?
- What are his biggest concerns?
- What other options is he considering?
- Is he more concerned about the money or about making a bad decision?
- What kind of work would he like to find? This would certainly be influenced by the online university's curriculum.
- What information does he need to help him make a decision?

While this person (aka "persona") doesn't actually exist, it's important not to make up details out of thin air. If in doubt about any part of this person's story, find some data to support it. Often, talking to a sales or customer support person will be very helpful. If you provide ratings and reviews on your site, read them all. Read your Facebook comments.

Be sure to address product features that are designed specifically for this persona. For instance, if you have a tuition financing program, have the customer commentary address the cost that this young man has on his mind. Would he qualify? Would he even try?

Some things just won't fit. For example, he may not be able to afford a smartphone, so he's not looking for a mobile experience. If you feel you need a mobile site, save that requirement for a different persona who would have a smartphone.

At this point, you may feel that you know this man. So give him a name. How about Julian?

List the Things They Need to Know

After hearing your persona talk about his story in such detail, it should be easy to list the things he needs to know to feel "comfortable and confident" taking action.

What information would you give Julian? He will have only a few overriding concerns:

- Does the school offer a course of study that he thinks he can learn?
- Can he get a good job after he graduates from the school?
- Can he pay the tuition?

A course catalog may not be enough for Julian. He's not coming to fulfill a dream, but to solve a financial problem. How can your site help him identify a course of study he can master?

The school's awards and prestige are not going to be of interest to Julian. However, if employers are interested in the school's awards and prestige, that will be very important to him.

Without the commentary, you might have assumed that price is the biggest issue for Julian. However, it may not be necessary to lead with information about the cost of tuition. Perhaps a discussion about programs that make the education affordable will be more effective.

These distinctions are important. Common sense tells us that a course catalog, credibility, and pricing are the most important things an online university can provide on their website. However, these are not the most important things to Julian.

Who'd have thought?

Now, look at the assumptions you've made for *your* site. How would customer commentaries change the types of information you provide? Where does common sense fall down?

A common mistake is to hold back *pricing*. This puts your visitors in the position of looking really stupid when they call and find out your solution is way out of their price range. This doesn't build confidence or comfort.

Make a list of things your best customer is looking for. Define what is really important to this person—not what you *think* he or she should want to know.

Pick a Mode of Research

Now ask yourself, "How does my best prospect like to do research online?"

Does she like to read reports, blog posts, or tweets?

Is she interested in what others buy, review, or rate?

Does she want third-party proof or testimonials that our solution is best?

Is she looking for a trusted expert, a friendly guide, or an elite brand?

Does she like video, audio, or webinars?

This exercise is important because it tells you how to craft and present content to your prime visitor.

Imagine a woman who has decided to remodel her bathroom. She will need a plumber. Her search will be methodical. A plumbing website may have to address references, time in business, insurance, and experience with certain materials.

Now imagine that the same woman just found a leak under her sink—a leak that is quickly ruining her wood floors. She isn't going to care how long a plumber has been in business. She won't be calling referrals. She won't ask about insurance. As soon as she finds a plumber who offers emergency service and provides a phone number, she is going to call. Period.

Same woman, two different "modes of research."

Bryan and Jeffrey Eisenberg literally wrote the book on online personas. In their best-seller *Waiting for Your Cat to Bark?* they present a simple map for what they call "modes of persuasion."

While these modes are based on Myers-Briggs research, the Eisenbergs have boiled things down to four. Think about your persona's customer commentary and ask two questions:

1. Will this visitor make decisions quickly, or deliberately?
2. Will he or she make a logical decision, or an emotional decision?

In the first scenario, our plumber-seeking woman was making a deliberate, logical decision. A lot of money was at stake, and she had time. In scenario two, however, she was in a frame of mind to make a quick and emotional decision.

Let's take a closer look at these four types of visitors.

The quick, logical researcher

These visitors are coming with a specific goal, but will take the time to be sure they're getting the best solution. They like to be in control and are looking for ways to complete tasks. Hit them quickly with a payoff. The headline of your landing page should give them a good benefit-laden reason to stay and explore.

The quick, emotional researcher

These visitors are just itching to take action. They will act quickly and abandon you quickly as well. They aren't going to look too hard before moving on. Give them something to do quickly and make it clear what they will get from taking action. Don't expect them to read much or even scroll the page.

The deliberate, logical researcher

These visitors don't take action until they know everything. They want to be the expert, and will need all of the details about all solutions before they feel comfortable calling or buying. They may provide their contact information in exchange for in-depth information.

The deliberate, emotional researcher

These visitors make decisions slowly. They will take action based on how your company and solutions make them feel. The "human touch" is very effective with these visitors, as relationships are very important to them.

Choose only one of these modes for each persona. This will keep your writers and designers from communicating in a neutral way. It will help your team imagine content to serve each persona according to the specific ways he or she likes to research.

What Do You Want Your Visitors to Do?

There are three actions a visitor can take. Let's take a look at each.

1. Buy Something with Cash

When your publication, online store, or online service has convinced someone to buy, your call to action must be stated in terms he can relate to. You've given him a reason to buy. Now, your writers and designers must *invite* him to buy.

To craft an effective call to action, your team must understand the persona and his mode of research. What words and images would be inviting to him?

If you have an online store and your persona is quick and emotional, you might want to place a message near the "Add to Cart" button, telling him his items can be "delivered within two days." This will be more appealing to this type of visitor than simply stating that an item is "in stock."

If you're a publication targeting a deliberate, emotional persona, he may be more likely to subscribe after hearing "We Want You to Join Us" instead of "Subscribe Now." Remember, it's all about relationships with this type of visitor.

2. Provide Contact Information and Permission to Continue a Conversation with You

Perhaps you need to ask the visitor to "buy" something with information—their contact information. This charges your subscriber battery.

Base the design of your "information products" on your persona's triggers, commentary, and mode of research. A logical and deliberate visitor may be interested in a report that details the steps of a process. A logical but quick-deciding visitor will want to know what makes your offering better. A quick and emotional decision maker may prefer a 30-second video. An emotional, deliberate visitor may want to see video featuring your employees describing your company and products.

Armed with your customer commentary and information about the persona's triggers and mode of research, your content development team will be well-prepared to deliver content that starts conversations—conversations that lead to sales.

3. Identify Themselves as Unqualified to Purchase What You Offer

Even though this action only requires that the visitor leave your site, this is where many web development teams fall down. They just don't want to let go.

Too often we feel the need to serve visitors who aren't ready to take action. We offer more links, more content, and more alternatives on our pages in a desperate attempt to keep them from leaving.

Let them go.

We're also afraid to say something powerful to our most qualified visitors, for fear of turning off others. This leads us to water down content, hide our company's personality, and bore everyone who visits.

If this describes your website, know this: Sooner or later, you're going to have to walk away from some of your visitors so you can speak more clearly to your best visitors.

In his book *The Wizard of Ads*, Roy H. Williams gave us his "nine secret words": *The risk of insult is the price of clarity.*

That said:

- Let people know who you are and don't apologize for it.
- If you're the more expensive solution, look expensive.
- If you're the cheapest, don't try to act top-shelf.
- If you're a small business, don't try to look big. You're not.
- Go ahead and talk about price, admit where your tradeoffs are, and then own the visitors who need and will pay for your offering. Let the rest go on with their lives.

Breathing Life into Your Rock Star Personas

If you feel a bit like a digital Dr. Frankenstein, it's because you are. The personas you have created here don't exist. They are scarecrows—figments of your knowledge.

And they will guide your team to higher and higher conversion rates.

The final step is to bring them to life.

Give Them Names

Choose names for your most cherished visitors. I chose Julian for our online university prospect.

Have a little fun. Choose names that bring each persona's general profile to mind, but that don't stereotype or diminish your empathy for them. Here are some examples:

- "Julian Newdad"
- "Frances Frantic"
- "Brian Bothered"
- "Erwin Earnest."

Flesh Out the Details

What kind of house does someone making $175,000 a year live in? Your copywriter may imagine a huge place in the nicest part of town. A high-paid marketing executive may wonder how anyone could own a home for so little. This difference in thinking highlights the limitations of demographics.

By themselves, demographics are subject to interpretation—and you cannot have the members of your team working with different interpretations.

Copywriters need to know at what level to write their prose, so education level is usually important. Beyond that, choose only the demographics they will need to craft content that speaks to your visitors. Common details include:

- Age
- Gender
- Income
- Family status
- Access to computers
- Internet access.

For businesspeople, you may also include:

- Company
- Title
- Job description
- Company size.

Other demographics that may or may not apply:

- ZIP code
- City, state, country
- Number and age of children
- Nationality
- Mobile phone ownership.

Again, include only those demographics that will alter your approach.

Give Them Faces

The best personas include a picture of the person. How do you get a picture of someone who doesn't exist? Consider some of the following sources. Try to capture the right look and attitude of the persona as you're looking through the options.

Use a picture from Flickr.

Flickr is a great source of Creative Commons-licensed images, which means you can use them as long as you adhere to the terms of the license. Try entering a few keywords into CompFight.com to find the right Flickr images.

Use Google, Bing, or Yahoo! Image Search.

Many of the images found on search engines are copyright-protected, but you should be able to find some that will be okay for internal use only.

Use a picture of a real customer.

If you have a real client who accurately reflects one of your personas, ask him for permission to use his photo. Be sure to adhere to your privacy policy, though. It may be inappropriate to share a client's image and name with the outside world.

Use stock photos as a last resort. These images are posed, artificial, and touched up. They'll distract from the empathy you're trying to build. If you have to use stock photos, choose images that are as realistic as possible.

Where Do You Keep All of This?

Writing down the details about personas is not difficult. Download my free Persona Template if you like by visiting our blog at CustomerCreationEquation.com.

Don't worry that if you record a persona in writing that it will be set in stone. Personas will naturally evolve as you learn more about your visitors. Some of your assumptions will be proven wrong. This is a good thing. You can make adjustments down the road.

No Experiment is a Failure as Long as You Learn Something From It

As your team spends more time working with personas, their conversations will change. Statements like "We should add titles from our blog posts to the home page" will turn to "Mike is going to want to drill down on some issues. We should put blog titles on the home page for him."

And when your team proposes new features, you'll all be able to ask: Who is this feature for? You'll make better decisions across the board when you're talking about "Mary," "Mike," and "Maurice," versus a "demographic segment."

Your portfolio of personas is a powerful tool. It represents what you know about your best customers. When everyone on your team understands the personas, they will be in a much better position to communicate in a way that resonates with your audience and moves them toward action. So go ahead and get everyone introduced—say hello to your visitors!

Conclusion

If I were to summarize the purpose of your journey through this book and toward online success, I would say that it is about **knowing versus thinking.**

You *thought* you knew what it took to build an effective website for your business. With your lab equipment, you now can *know* what works and what doesn't.

I *think* I've given you some very reliable best practices for online strategy, content marketing, list development, social media, landing pages and home pages. My recommendations may not work for your particular audience. If I'm wrong, you will *know* because you now can measure your online strategies right down to the lead, subscriber, or sale.

If I've done my job here, you should have had at least one of your previous assumptions dashed. This is the rule of the scientific method: The data will tell you stories you may find hard to believe. These are the unexpected formulas.

Unexpected Formula #1.	Your opinion doesn't matter.
Unexpected Formula #2.	Your visitors don't care about your company or your products.
Unexpected Formula #3.	Your visitors will tell you exactly what to do.
Unexpected Formula #4.	Conversion is about more than landing pages, buttons, forms, and shopping carts.
Unexpected Formula #5.	Every click is a promise that you must keep.
Unexpected Formula #6.	Every change is an experiment.
Unexpected Formula #7.	Specifics are the hallmark of conversion.
Unexpected Formula #8.	Don't copy your competitors.
Unexpected Formula #9.	Market research is a collection of hypotheses, not answers.

Unexpected Formula #10.	Don't send your store-bought traffic to social networks.
Unexpected Formula #11.	The most important part of a design is the dollars it generates.
Unexpected Formula #12.	Store the attention you've paid for and use it again and again.
Unexpected Formula #13.	The most valuable use of a blog is as a content source.
Unexpected Formula #14.	Start at the end when designing your landing pages.
Unexpected Formula #15.	Sometimes it's okay—even preferable—if visitors abandon you.
Unexpected Formula #16.	Email is the biggest social network on the planet—bigger and more effective even than Facebook.
Unexpected Formula #17.	Business people are still people and should be treated as such.
Unexpected Formula #18.	The job of your home page is to get people off of your home page.
Unexpected Formula #19.	Your audience is unique—question what people like me tell you about optimizing.
Unexpected Formula #20.	You will find your own surprises as you continue on this journey.

Several of these should assault your sensibilities and lead you to question my sanity. The good news is that you don't have to take my word for it. You now have the tools that will make you a better decision maker on the web. You are now in a position to ask your team the tough questions, and to know which answers are the right ones.

If nothing else, you should realize that you have to question the "experts."

Ideally, the journey you started here will take you to a place where conversion becomes a natural part of your business. For every campaign, program, and article they produce, your team will ask, "What can we expect from this?" and "How can we measure that?" They'll want to try multiple versions of your pages, emails, ads, and content. Everyone will have a basic understanding of analytics and the scientific method.

Ultimately, your business will boom as your team begins to truly understand the people engaging with your business online. An enlightened team will be able to "deliver the gifts" of your business to your customers, who will reward you with their hard-earned money and loyalty.

There is more to be done—and more cool toys to play with. Join in on the conversations and take advantage of additional resources at the Customer Creation Equation Blog (CustomerCreationEquation.com).

Welcome to this new path. Enjoy your success.

References

Chapter 1

Graves, Philip. Consumer.ology: *The Market Research Myth, the Truth about Consumers and the Psychology of Shopping.* Nicholas Brealey Publishing, 2010.

Chapter 4

Nielsen Company. "Top 10 Online Retailers by Conversion Rate – March 2010." May 3, 2010.
http://www.marketingcharts.com/direct/top-10-online-retailers-by-conversion-rate-march-2010-12774/

Chapter 6

Gladwell, Malcolm. *Outliers: The Story of Success.* Little, Brown and Company, 2008.

Robbins, Tom. *Fierce Invalids Home From Hot Climates.* Bantam, 2001.

Interview: Rico Naso, Zappos.com. http://www.youtube.com/watch?v=ry5LqTLaegE

Chapter 7

Ariely, Dan. *Predictably Irrational: The Hidden Forces That Shape Our Decision.* Harper Perennial, rev. 2010.

Cialdini, Robert B. *Influence: The Psychology of Persuasion.* Collins, revised 1998.

Chapter 8

Cialdini, Robert B. *Influence: Science and Practice.* Prentice Hall, 5th edition, 2008.

Chapter 9

Mulpuru, Sucharita and Hult, Peter. *Understanding Shopping Cart Abandonment.* Forrester Research, May 2010.
http://www.forrester.com/Understanding+Shopping+Cart+Abandonment/fulltext/-/E-RES56827

Chapter 10

Ash, Tim. *Landing Page Optimization: The Definitive Guide to Testing and Tuning for Conversions.* Wiley Publishing, 2008.

Coker, Brent, Ph.D. "Prettier websites make for more trusting web surfers, study finds." University of Melbourne. July 2011. http://newsroom.melbourne.edu/news/n-575

Chapter 11

Bitly. "You just shared a link. How long will people pay attention?" Blog post. September 6, 2011. http://bit.ly/nu7IDw

Godin, Seth. *Tribes: We Need You to Lead Us.* Portfolio Hardcover, 1 edition. 2008.

Solis, Brian. *Engage! The Complete Guide for Brands and Businesses to Build, Cultivate, and Measure Success in the New Web.* Wiley Publishing, 2010.

Solis, Brian. "Opportunity Clicks: Social Media and Converting Clicks into Action." Blog post. February 23, 2011. http://www.briansolis.com/2011/02/opportunity-clicks-social-media-and-converting-clicks-into-action/

Sysomos. "Replies and Retweets on Twitter." September 2010. http://www.sysomos.com/insidetwitter/engagement/

Zarrella, Dan. *Zarrella's Hierarchy of Contagiousness: The Science, Design, and Engineering of Contagious Ideas.* The Domino Project, 2011.

Zarrella, Dan. "5 Scientifically Proven Ways to Get More ReTweets." Blog post. July 26, 2011. http://danzarrella.com/infographic-5-scientifically-proven-ways-to-get-more-retweets.html#

Chapter 12

Eisenberg, Bryan and Eisenberg, Jeffrey. *Waiting for Your Cat to Bark? Persuading Customers When They Ignore Marketing.* Thomas Nelson, 2006.

Williams, Roy H. *The Wizard of Ads: Turning Words into Magic and Dreamers into Millionaires.* Bard Press, 1998.

Acknowledgments

I've never had an original thought in my life. Everything I know is borrowed or stolen from someone far brighter than myself.

Most notable among my victims are Bryan and Jeffrey Eisenberg, whose ideas on the development and application of personas will change your website. I built my practice on their concepts and probably owe them a great deal in royalty payments. Please don't tell them about this book.

Dave Evans has been an inspiration and a partner in projects that probed online trends. Dave knows how to find value in all things. He also introduced me to the fine folks at ClickZ, who gave me my first "real" writing job.

Most of the material in this book was gestated as speeches and presentations. To all those trusting souls who let me present, write, and extemporize for them before they had any evidence that I wouldn't embarrass them, I offer my heartfelt gratitude – and my sincerest apology for ultimately embarrassing them. Of note are InnoTech's Sean Lowery, PubCon's Brett Tabke, and the folks at Search Engine Land.

Volacci's Ben Finklea was midwife to the birth of conversion science. Apogee Results' Bill Leake helped me realize what these disciplines were worth in the marketplace, so that conversion science could flourish. The Wizard Academy and Roy H. Williams showed me that communicating well is the most noble of arts.

To Joe Pulizzi, who offered to publish this book over at Patsy's Café in south Austin, I am very grateful. Joe must have seen more in me than the plate of chicken fried steak I had just finished.

To the often bewildered team that somehow made this book a reality, I extend the warmest of gratitude. Lisa Murton Beets, Newt Barrett, Shelly Koenig, Promote A Book's Michael Drew, and all the folks at the Content Marketing Institute who somehow guided me through the process of turning whim and fancy into organized thought.

To my clients, who have been the guinea pigs in our conversion lab, I've learned as much as you have through your bravery and your commitment to your visitors.

Finally, to the owners of the thousands of blogs, reports, and case studies I've read over the years, you have inspired this book through your amazing writing and generosity. Please, if you recognize any of your ideas or concepts in this work, take the credit due and add your name here.

_____

_____

_____

_____

_____

About Brian Massey

Brian Massey,
The Conversion Scientist™

Brian Massey is The Conversion Scientist™ at Conversion Sciences (ConversionScientist.com) and he has the lab coat to prove it. His rare combination of interests, experience, and neuroses was developed over almost 20 years as a computer programmer, entrepreneur, corporate marketer, national speaker, and writer.

"Conversion" is the process of converting web traffic to leads and sales, and Conversion Sciences brings this ability to businesses of all sizes.

Brian's mission is to change the Internet from a giant digital brochure stand to a place where problems are solved and dreams are fulfilled. He's helped dozens of businesses transform their sites through a steady diet of visitor profiling, purposeful content, analytics, and testing.

"There are websites that make you feel like they were built just for you," he says. "Is yours one of these? It could be."

Brian's presentations and workshops have been characterized as "memorable" and he can be heard at conferences and in board rooms everywhere. From his digital conversion lab, he transmits via The Conversion Scientist website and through his columns at ClickZ.com, Search Engine Lane (SearchEngineLand.com), and the Content Marketing Institute (ContentInstitute.com).

Brian lives and works in Austin, Texas, where life and the Internet are hopelessly entwined.

Conversion Sciences Grows Online Businesses

There are places on the web that are instantly familiar … places that make you feel as if they were built specifically with your needs in mind. Is your website one of these? It could be.

Conversion Sciences is a team of geeks and creatives who work on sites like yours to make them places where visitors feel confident taking action—in other words, sites that grow business. No matter how sophisticated you may be now, we have a place for you to plug into the conversion journey.

Just starting out? Continue your study of conversion practices at
www.CustomerCreationEquation.com

Building your own digital conversion laboratory? Start at
www.MyConversionLab.com

If you have the tools, we can provide some nice people in clean white coats to put those tools to work for you. Our services are detailed at
www.ConversionSciences.com

Our goals for your business are simple:

- Ring up more revenue from the visitors to your site
- Slash the cost of getting advertising and marketing
- Entice return visits from prospects and customers alike
- Choreograph your advertising, social media, email, and search with your site so they work together.

If you are not yet a subscriber to *The Conversion Scientist*, our free weekly guide to smart websites, sign up at
www.ConversionScientist.com.

Or, get a jump on adding some science to your site and contact us right now. We're waiting to hear from you.

Conversion Sciences, LLC
Measure. Mix. Maximize.
Scientist direct: (888) 961-6604
By email: Hello@ConversionSciences.com
On the web: www.ConversionSciences.com

Are You Letting the 5 Myths of Video for Business Hold You Back?

1. Professional video is too expensive.
2. Videos may not work for our products or services.
3. Our customers don't want video.
4. Any video is better than no video, no matter what.
5. It's too hard to get approval and buy-in from management.

The truth is, companies are using video to accelerate their online sales in almost every industry.

Conversion Sciences Video Science is a video pilot service that debunks the myths of product video and drives huge increases in revenue.

1. Learn how video can be applied to any product or service with great results.
2. Discover the actual increase in sales that will pay for your videos.
3. Identify the segments of your visitors that will vote for video with their dollars.
4. Use optimization techniques to create and test different video variations and learn the exact videos that work for your audience BEFORE your scale your program.
5. Get the sales data that makes video an obvious choice for your business.

Discover the video formula that will make your visitors *convert*.

Request your free analysis.

http://conversionsciences.com/video

Scientist Direct: **888-961-6604**

Sci-mail: **video@conversionsciences.com**

Conversion Sciences, LLC

Index

CPSIA information can be obtained at www.ICGtesting.com
Printed in the USA
LVOW13s2031050814

397484LV00013B/339/P